"Let's Get Changed Lads"

developing work with boys and young men

Trefor Lloyd

First published 1997

by Working with Men

320 Commercial Way, London SE15 1QN

©1997 @ Trefor Lloyd

Layout, Design and Printed by

RAP, 201 Spotland Road, Rochdale OL12 7AF

ISBN: 1 900468 03 4

Content

Acknowledgements

Many people have contributed to the production and the ideas within this book. I am indebted to all of those who, over the years, have been bold enough to develop their practice with boys and young men, making use of our growing understanding of masculinity. Without them, this book would have no purpose and little content. Thanks to all of you - you know who you are.

More specifically, thank you to Paul Allen, Mohamed Aslam, Sylvan Baker, Carl Balshaw, Paul Brown, Tommy Dallas, Mike Farnfield, Ken Harland, Khalid Abdul Karim Mair, Mark Price, Chris Reed and Jim Rowe, who all enthusiastically contributed examples of practice; to Steve Bolger and Mike Farnfield for their very useful comments on the anti-sexist work chapter; to John Moore for his comments on the masculinity chapter and Grant Biddle for his contribution to the resources section. To Neil Davidson for our long and always-developing work partnership and friendship, who has thoughtfully commented on drafts of this book; and to Tristan Wood for his excellent and respectful editing, giving it his usual skill and commitment, in spite of other pressures on his time.

This book is dedicated to the memory of Albert Lloyd, and to the futures of Ben Lloyd Ennals and Arun Khoot Lloyd.

Foreword

The position of boys and young men in our society today has become a matter of concern to practitioners as well as policy makers. During the last decade, we have seen a startling level of social change. There has also been a huge rise in unemployment, increasing rates of divorce, changes in the transition from school to work, altered rules for benefits and social security payments, and a decrease in resources available for young people generally. Many have taken the view that males have been more affected than females by these changes.

To take employment as one example, the withering away of manufacturing industry and the growth in service industries has undoubtedly made the entry into the labour market easier for young women and harder for young men. In education, girls are doing better in school-based examinations, especially at GCSE level. A number of alternative explanations have been put forward to explain this, and we cannot be certain what lies at the heart of the gender difference. What is clear, however, is that the school environment is not providing the stimulus and opportunity for boys that was once the case.

In the mental health arena, the suicide rates among young men in Britain have risen since the early 1980's, in contrast to the rates among young women which have stayed relatively stable. Again, no one simple explanation is possible, but such a trend must reflect increasing distress and alienation among this group in our society.

If we are to take seriously the needs of young men in the context of the social changes which they are experiencing in the late 1990's, then we urgently need some practical guidelines for work in this area. There is no group offering a more positive model of such an approach than Working With Men. WWM - in spite of being a very small organisation - has provided some outstanding examples of good practice over the last few years, and Trefor Lloyd, the author of this book, has been a key figure in the group's development.

There has been much hand-wringing over the way we bring up our male children today. The lack of role models; the absence of some fathers because of family breakdown, or because of long hours at work; the violence in the media and on the streets - all these may play a part in creating a climate of perceived damage or neglect. We should, as a matter of urgency, be considering how to redress the balance. We should be looking for constructive ways to assist young men towards adulthood in a changing society. I believe this book provides a timely, informative and inspiring example of what can be done. I am delighted to be able to recommend it to the widest possible audience.

John Coleman

Introduction

Gender relations are changing at a pace. Women are continuing to enter the labour market, sport, clubs and other environments thought previously to belong to men. Some of the internal expectations that women have been harbouring are becoming the social reality. Feminism (and other pro-women ideologies) has raised women's expectations that the world is theirs. More women are in work, women's intolerance of male violence has increased, women are initiating the majority of divorces, and serious discussions about whether women need men are increasingly commonplace. But, what about men?

Their social environment is certainly changing. Opportunities for 'men's jobs' have reduced substantially and are very unlikely to return. Our historical fallback for men's unemployment – war – has gone (hopefully, never to return) and increasingly questions about 'the male identity' and what the future holds for men, are being added to old chestnuts such as "How can we stop young men's deviance?". The debate has a number of variations; for writers such as Neil Lyndon and Warren Farrall [1] men are the new victims, for Keith Pringle and Jeff Hearn [2] power and male dominance are the issues to be focused on, while Campbell and Phillips [3] are concerned about the time bomb nature of the problems of male identity, especially for young men. All of these writers (and many others currently writing about men) contribute a range of perspectives that make up the complex picture that is masculinities.

On a more popular front, the media prefer to bring us the new statistics (employment, for example, with case studies and quotes from 'experts'), specific issues about men's health, crime, underachievement and fatherhood, or tasty conflict such as the 'sex wars' debate of the early 90's, or whether women need, or want, men. Whether men are redundant has moved from a bit of fun to a serious question.

The last few years have seen a steady increase in the level of media and academic interest in men. Questions and problems have been raised, many of the issues and trends identified, the concerns and fears voiced and a level of understanding reached, but the question "What can we do about it?" has rarely been asked let alone answered. Weighing heavily behind many of the media debates and academic studies are serious questions about whether men are able and/or willing to change. For Pringle and Hearn, men must be made to change (they are too dangerous unless they do), although they will be resistant because of the power they have. For Lyndon and Farrell, the change needs to be with society's attitudes and laws and the roles expected of men (victim politics always focuses on the responsibility of the other). For the more psychological texts, men have difficulties with change because they can't communicate, can't express their feelings, don't recognise their inner selves, etc., etc. Interestingly, when men's ability and willingness to change are discussed, invariably the discussion takes a negative edge. Within a work area such as the criminal justice system, tensions arise about whether we lead with a stick or a carrot. With crime being such a male preserve, do we punish or rehabilitate, do we see the offender as perpetrator (of the crime) or victim (of, for example, the government's economic policy); are men to be made accountable for their actions or empathised with? These and many other polar positions are bread and butter to criminal justice workers, but they reflect a deep seated uncertainty as to whether men will change if invited to do so, or whether they will only change if forced, cajoled and banged up!

This book is primarily about how we can develop services,

programmes and styles of work that are men friendly, that engage with the question "What can we do about it?" at a very practical level. Our experience within Working With Men is that there is a rapidly growing interest in theory and practice in a number of welfare fields, notably youthwork, teaching, health and criminal justice, especially in terms of working with boys and young men.

This book aims to meet this growing interest by reviewing the current theoretical approaches (in terms of their usefulness to practice); by suggesting a theory/practice model that can help professional workers develop their practice; and by reviewing practice issues that workers are using to enable boys and young men to change and develop. The first part concentrates on the statistical and research data currently available which help us understand what is happening to young men. The various perspectives on masculinity are then reviewed, along with the process of transition (from boyhood to manhood) which has provoked the interest of academics and practitioners alike. This first part concludes with a review of the implications that these understandings and theoretical perspectives have for work with boys.

Part Two addresses the development of practice with young men. This includes a review of the different practice issues implicit in Part One, followed by a series of examples of practice. It concludes with a resource list that will be of use to workers developing their work with boys and young men.

While that describes the contents, this book builds on and follows a number of strands and viewpoints that are important in understanding and developing good practice with young men. These strands and positions include:

1. The tension between the (external) social environment and the (internal) mindset – the contrast between the rapidly changing circumstances that young men are finding themselves in, and the ways they have been taught to think

they ought to live their lives, are increasingly at odds with each other. So, for example, if young men have a deep-seated belief that, as a man, their role is to be a bread winner, but they find themselves with very few opportunities to fulfil this belief, then this will create internal conflict. Role strain, as Pleck has called it[4], is highest when the external and internal differences are at their most extreme.

2. The inter-relationship between these internal and external factors. Not only do we want to understand what is happening to young men, but we also want to know how we can intervene in a positive way. While much of the literature to date has concentrated on identifying and understanding what is happening, we want to grapple with understanding to enable us to grapple with intervention.

3. Young men continuing to be offered rigid constructions of masculinity. Being a bread winner still provides the primary identity for many young men in terms of what it is to be a man.

4. Some workers' attitudes, approaches and views of young men being a barrier to the development of men friendly services. These attitudes often include a view that men can't, or won't, change. Workers often say that they "just don't understand why he did what he did", or "Boys won't respond to the opportunities offered; they just want to muck around".

5. Masculinity, gender, sexism, patriarchy and sexuality are different and overlapping concepts which can't be used interchangeably. Together, they make up a complex (and sometimes contradictory) picture of relationships between men and women, men and men, and women and women.

6. Masculinity is not a negative concept. Too much of the debate about masculinity is problematic, but any model of practice must be built on a positive view of the group it is

targeted at to make it useful and effective. A positive view of boys and young men is essential to enable workers to intervene effectively, whether the curriculum is work, their future, or sexism.

These and other themes will be regularly returned to throughout this volume and are highlighted here for the reader to identify the perspective and intentions this book has. As mentioned already, this book is about developing practice. It aims to encourage and enable workers to understand boys, young men and masculinity, to help them to develop useful and effective practice that involves and values young men and the issues they have, and will continue to have to deal with in their lives.

Because the book is made up of two distinct, but interlinked parts, this may determine how you approach it. This will, in part, reflect how you approach ideas and the relationship between theory and practice. If you 'lead' with theory, like to mull over the concepts, chew over the perspectives and understand the context before you reflect on your's and others' practice, then you will want to start at the beginning and proceed. If, however, you are first and foremost a practitioner, who addresses issues as and when they emerge in your practice, you may want to turn to Part Two and even start with the examples of practice. The order of these parts has been determined by common form, rather than any suggestion that context is more important than practice, or that contextual issues must be grappled with and addressed first. In short, do not be constrained by tradition, or how a book 'should' be read. On reflection, this is probably one of the most important underlying principles of this book — do not be constrained by traditional (or any other form of) masculinity, think afresh and let this book stimulate you in the development of your work. But, most of all, enjoy!

References

1. Lyndon N. No More Sex Wars: The failures of feminism Mandarin, London, 1992. Farrall W. The Myth of Male Power (why men are the disposable sex) Fourth Estate, London, 1993.

2. Pringle K. Men, Masculinities & Social Welfare UCL Press, London, 1995. Hearn J. & Morgan D. (eds.) Men, Masculinities and Social Theory Unwin Hyman, London, 1990.

3. Campbell B. Goliath (Britain's Dangerous Places) Methuen, London, 1993. Phillips A. The Trouble With Boys (parenting the men of the future) Pandora, London, 1993.

4. Pleck J. The Myth of Masculinity MIT Press, Cambridge, MA, 1981.

Part One

Understanding Boys and Young Men

What is happening to young men?

In our attempt to understand what is happening to young men, we begin by reviewing the statistical and research data. For some readers, the mere mention of statistics may cause you to move on to the next chapter. With this tendency in mind, I have tried to make the data as accessible as possible. This chapter is structured around a number of key areas that impact on men generally, and on boys and young men in particular, and provides a crucial part of the context of why the development of work with young men is so important at this time.

The chapter is divided into two sections. The first reflects the changing context of young men's lives, the changes in employment, education, health and crime, while the second reflects the internal impact that these factors may be having on the mental health of young men. The internal/external distinction made in the Introduction, and the tension within the role strain model between the social environment and the internal mindset, are reflected here in terms of statistical and social trends and also research-based studies looking at the impact some of these trends may be having on young men.

Employment

Dramatic changes have taken place, and are continuing to occur, in the employment market. We will, in 1998, become the first European country to have a workforce which is 51% female. Since 1979, the number of men and women employed has changed dramatically:

in employment	1979	1994	%
Men	13.1m	10.9m	16.8
Women	9.4m	10.7m	+12.2(1)

From 1979 to 1994, there has been a 16.8% drop in the number of men in employment and a 12.2% increase in the number of women. Researchers monitoring these changes have estimated that 90% of the jobs created in this period have been seen as 'women's work' (low pay, part time, requiring small fingers), and a similar percentage of jobs lost were 'men's jobs' (wages high enough to keep a family, particularly manual or skilled labour). While unemployment for men is, of course, not new, such dramatic changes in the workforce have not been seen since industrialisation, and the gender changes are certainly unprecedented in the modern era.

Although fewer men are working, the actual number of hours they work has continued to increase, with those men working full time in 1994 averaging 45.4 hours a week (with women averaging 40.4 and both averages being higher than our European counterparts') [2].

Unemployment rates for young people have continued to rise, particularly for young men:

| | 1991 | | 1995 | |
	male	female	male	female
16-19 years	16.5%	13.2%	19.6%	14.8%
20-29 years	12.3%	9.4%	14.0%	9.2% [3]

Looking at the duration of unemployment, more young men appear in groups experiencing over 6 months':

| | males | | females | |
	16-19	20-29	16-19	20-29
less than 3 months	39.9%	18.6%	40.7%	32.8%
3 6 months	19.4%	16.4%	22.5%	18.9%
6 months to 1 year	22.4%	19.9%	22.1%	18.8%
1 2 years	13.5%	18.7%	11.1%	14.6%
2 3 years	9.3%	6.2%		
3 years or more	17.0%	8.7%		

There are over 3 males to 1 female aged 18-24 years who have been unemployed for a year or more. In fact, the longer the period of unemployment, the wider the gap between men and women [3].

Gender is one of the most important factors in recent employment statistics. Male unemployment continues to increase (from 9.2% in 1991 to 10.1% in 1995), but, even more significantly, the types of jobs that pay 'a man's wage' (enough to keep a family) and those that are thought to be 'manly jobs' (heavy industry and hard physical labour) are in rapid decline. Routes into these jobs (apprenticeships) have, of course, reduced as well, impacting on young men in both the short and long term [3].

The more unskilled a man is, the more likely he is to be unemployed. According to a Labour Party analysis of official figures [4], up to 40% of men without qualifications are out of work, and the numbers are growing.

The unemployment rate for black and men is even higher than for white men:

	males	females
White	8%	5%
African Caribbean and African	21%	14%
Indian	10%	7%
Pakistani and Bangladeshi	18%	7% [3]

The unemployment rate for 16-24-year old black males in London is 62%, with young black men three times more likely to be jobless than young white men [2].

The implications of these figures are that either we need to create large numbers of jobs that young men perceive as 'men's jobs', or engage with young men about their beliefs and assumptions about what constitutes men's and women's work and their views about being bread winners. Assumptions that young men may have about filling a sole bread winner role, given the current trends, need careful scrutiny, as the numbers of men with this role are rapidly declining. A further implication is that an increasingly large number of young men do not have access to the symbols of manhood (clothes, cars, drinking) that employment, status and money bring.

Health

Two major concerns have been raised about young men's health. They are the steady rise in suicides and the level of risks young men are prepared to take. While suicide rates have been steadily decreasing since the mid-seventies for women, there has been a corresponding increase for men especially young men. Men from social classes I and V are most likely to commit suicide, as are unemployed men (2-3 times); single, divorced and widowed men (3 times); men with AIDS; men in prison; or abusers of alcohol and drugs [5].

While the reasons for this increase appear to be multi faceted, a number of commentators have suggested that employment changes and the rapidly changing role for men have at least contributed [6], as have men's difficulties in asking for help and expressing their feelings [7].

The Chief Medical Officer, in his annual report of 1992 [8], suggested that:

"Although some diseases, such as prostatism, are obviously unique to men, the main differences in mortality and morbidity relate to variations in exposure to risk factors".

Risk is a recurrent theme in the statistics about young men. Boys under 5 years of age are thought to be more at risk of accidents, because of their "more active and physical forms of play", their "higher levels of inquisitiveness" and the "expectations of parents about boys that they will be more adventurous" [9].

Accidents, while only accounting for 1.9% of all male deaths in 1991, reflect 42% of all deaths of 15-24-year olds, and

17% of deaths of 25-44-year old men. Risk taking behaviour, combined with lack of experience, alcohol and (to a lesser extent) drugs, are significant factors in accidents for this age group. In addition to deaths, an estimated 10,000 children a year are left with long term health problems from accidents: a large proportion of these are male [10]. Boys are twice as likely as girls to have an accident, with girls thought to be better at spotting dangers and less likely to trip, fall or bump into things [11].

In 1995, 27% of men over the age of 16 years drank more than the recommended level of 21 units a week, with 14% drinking at least 36 units per week. These men were spread fairly evenly over all socio-economic groups [12]. Over a third of 18-24 year-olds drink over the recommended level [13]. These statistics beg the question, "Why do men take such risks?".

Crime

77% of 10-17-year-olds committing indicable offences (in England and Wales) are male, with 85.6% of those aged 18-20 also male. 41.9% of criminal acts involve young men under the age of 21 years.

The majority of those found guilty or cautioned for indictable offences are accused of theft or handling stolen goods:

10-13 years of age	60%	(13,680)
14-17 years of age	47%	(37,882)
18-20 years of age	36%	(27,108)

followed by burglary:

10-13 years of age	18%
14-17 years of age	17%
18-20 years of age	13%

While general levels of indicable offences for these age groups have reduced substantially, the proportion of males to females remains the same.

The number of male drug addicts notified to the Home Office has gone up threefold, with the 21 to 30 year group increasing even more. 77.7% of all addicts, and 72% of those under 30 years of age, were male [13].

	1983	1993
All registered drug addicts	2979	8981
Those aged 21 to 30 years	1562	5058

Young people (young men) suffering from addiction to drink or drugs are thought to be responsible for more than one third of all solved burglaries, thefts and property crimes [14].

A survey has shown that some young offenders spend between £150 and £600 a week on drugs, yet more than half of them are unemployed, and nearly half have no financial support. Most of the young people aged between 15 and 24 in three penal institutions confessed to researchers that crime was their main source of income [15].

Over three quarters of victims of violent crime are male, of which more than 43% are victims of either pub or street brawls, while 32% of females are victims of domestic violence [16]. In the age group 16-29, 14.5% of all men have been victims of violence, compared to 8.3% of women. [17]

One in three men born in 1953 had been convicted of a serious offence by the age of 30. Most of their first convictions occurred at the age of 17; males first convicted in their early teens are more likely to continue offending than those convicted later [18].

Crime is, and always has been, a male preserve, but masculinity has rarely been considered as a contributing factor. The male preponderance has either been taken as fact (and not questioned) or raised as a possible biological reason for male criminality. DNA, brain size, testosterone and men's 'natural' aggression have all been considered as primary factors [19]. Masculinity remains a periphery factor in most criminologists' minds [20].

Education

There have been recent concerns about the differences in the educational achievements for boys and girls, with girls outperforming boys on most levels. While there has been some debate as to whether this is down to girls' achievement or boys' underachievement [21], there do seem to be reasons for concern about boys:

In 1993:	Boys%	Girls%
Achieved 5 top grades	39	48
3 or more A levels	14	15
University population	47	53
Graduates in work within 6 months	42	45
Still unemployed after a year	12	8 [22]

This would appear to be a recent development: if we compare figures for 1980/1 and 1993/4, in many groups females have started from a lower base and passed the males by:

	males		females	
	1980/1	1993/4	1980/1	1993/4
3 or more 'A' levels	10%	14%	8%	15%
1 or more 'A' levels	16%	21%	15%	23%
5 or more GCSE A C	24%	39%	26%	48%
1 or more GCSE A C	50%	64%	55%	75%[23]

Looking at specific subject areas, even in the traditional 'male' subjects females are doing well:

For GCSE grades A C	males		females	
	1988/9	1993/4	1988/9	1993/4
English	38%	45%	53%	62%
Any science	35%	43%	33%	43%
Mathematics	36%	42%	32%	42%
History	16%	18%	18%	24%[23]

The problems seem to develop far earlier than at GCSE stage, with males showing lower achievement rates in most teacher-assessed and tested areas. So, for example, for 7 year olds:

Teachers	assessment		Tests	
	males	females	males	females
Handwriting	76%	87%	76%	85%
Reading	76%	85%	76%	85%
Spelling	67%	80%	65%	77%
Writing	64%	76%	61%	74%
All elements	75%	85%[23]		

Boys make up two-thirds of children with learning difficulties; four-fifths of pupils expelled from school; and five-sixths of those with behavioural and discipline problems[23]. African-Caribbean boys are four times more likely to be excluded from school than white boys. African-Caribbean children represent 8.1% of all excluded children, while comprising only 2% of the school population[24].

The Impact on Young Men

The picture these selected statistics provide is a worrying one, with more young men finding themselves out of work, more likely to take risks with their health, get hurt in accidents, commit suicide, take drugs and drink to a harmful level, and end up with a long term disability at a young age. While crime is clearly a male preserve, research suggests that a large proportion of young crime is carried out by a small percentage of the male population. In education, in terms of exam results, university entrances and post-university jobs, young women are out-performing the young men.

How much these external factors are impacting on all young men is more difficult to assess. How much educational under-achievement, unemployment, health risks and criminal activity are reflections of the lives of a small, but significant, group of young men is hard to gauge. Certainly, some groups of young men may be appearing in at least three of these categories. Class, race and poverty have been suggested as significant factors impacting on young men's lives. The employment, health and education trends are certainly impacting on an ever-increasing number of young men.

In part, at least, the nature of being a man in the 90's has clearly altered, mainly because of these external, societal changes. But what evidence do we have that suggests that young men are concerned, or, indeed, struggling with this new environment? While this is harder to gauge, some research suggests that, for at least some groups of young men, the impact may be substantial.

Employment

The experience of unemployment has been shown to destroy men's personal and social identity (especially their 'breadwinner' identity), often resulting in a life crisis, with the inevitable increase in stress; leading to more families being poor; to effects on diet and other basic needs; and inevitably to illness. Long standing illness is 40% higher amongst unemployed men, compared to men in work. Other studies have shown a deterioration in men's mental health when unemployed, with an improvement if they return to work [25]. With such high levels of unemployment for young men, how will they react to this experience? Will they adapt, or will they struggle?

Health

Research has shown that the male gender role leads men to ignore their health needs. Explanations for the higher mortality rates for men have included levels of risk taking, "the outcome of differential risks acquired from role, stress, lifestyle, and preventative health practices. Psycho-social factors, how men and women perceive and evaluate symptoms, and their readiness and ability to take therapeutic action" [26].

When over 20,000 young people were asked, "If you wanted to share health problems, to whom would you probably turn?", 12.8% of 12 year old boys answered, "No one" (with only 6.9% of girls answering similarly), and, by 15 years of age, this response had risen to 13.8% (5.8% of girls). When asked, "When you have a problem, what do you do about it?", 18.8% of 12 year old boys answered that they "do nothing" [27].

Rutter and Smith[28] suggest that it is not so much social disadvantage as social dislocation which explains the dramatic rise in psycho-social disorders in young people. Family conflict and breakdown, the blocked pathways to attaining adult status and accompanying prolonged dependency on parents, the emergence of a distinctive and separate youth culture, and rising expectations which, too often, are left unfulfilled are all in interlocking ways? more likely causes of psycho-social disorders. It is this lengthening adolescence, status insecurity and uncertain personal identity which produces internal conflicts and clashes with parents and other authority figures and leads to self destructive behaviour by the young.

A number of studies have demonstrated a positive relationship between psychological masculinity and measures of mental health[29]. Most use the Bem Sex Role Inventory and/or the Personal Attributes Questionnaires which both measure 'positive' aspects of masculinity and femininity. Others have focused on more 'negative' aspects, such as emotional inexpression[30], and have found a strong relationship with mental health problems. Men who take on behaviour thought to be 'feminine' are thought by others to be 'less than men', whether it is because of 'self disclosure' [31] or holding 'female' jobs, such as nursing [32]. This can lead to lower self-esteem and gender role conflict and strain[33]. "Gender role conflict is a negative psychological state that results from the contradictory and/or unrealistic demands of the gender role"[33]. Davis and Walsh[34] found that there was a strong association between gender role conflict and both low self-esteem and anxiety.

Reviewing biological, psychological and social factors, Kilmartin[35] concluded that "males experienced a disproportionate number of childhood disorders, for example, attention deficit hyperactivity disorder and conduct disorder. Males constitute a majority of substance abusers, sexual deviants and people with behaviour control problems such as pyromania, compulsive gambling, and angry outbursts. More men than women are diagnosed as paranoid, antisocial, narcissistic and schizoid, and, of course, men are more likely to commit suicide".

Education

Boys aged 11 to 16 are twice as likely as girls to be unhappy and disillusioned at school, twice as likely to truant, do no homework and misbehave in lessons [36]. Boys outnumber girls 2:1 in Britain's schools for children with learning difficulties. In special units for behavioural problems, there are six boys for every girl [37].

"It is a feature common in the playgrounds of every school in the country. Boys play football; the girls are busy talking to each other… expectations and social conditioning play a very important role in shaping the performance of children". Girls are thought to be more willing to talk, or sit down and read, which helps improve their English. Some have suggested that we must start giving boys the same encouragement (and also discipline) as girls. "Boys find it easier to be labelled as a nuisance and disruptive, rather than thick". The ironic twist is that boys are more likely to believe they are bright, even though their performance at GCSE lags well behind girls' [38].

Boys tend to get more negative responses than girls. There is an assumption they are going to be naughty. The boys feel that it is alright for girls to work hard, but not for themselves if they want to appear cool and 'be a lad'. Some studies have suggested that boys are worried by the new assertiveness of girls; that, when they are by themselves, they have no one to show off to, making teaching easier [39]. The revolution in girls' education has had a price: demoralisation of boys. Boys have become so pessimistic that their depression is affecting their academic performance [40].

These studies suggest that the external changes affecting young men's lives are impacting on their internal selves and vice versa. Mental and physical illness, a perceived loss of status, disruptive and withdrawn behaviour, psycho-social disorders, violence, suicide and further risk-taking may all be manifestations of internal difficulties being experienced by young men.

However, the picture we have of young men's internal struggles remains very limited. Of course, the nature of being a man for many includes the need to be self sufficient, tough enough to deal with anything and in control of emotions not the pre-requisites for discussions about the effects of unemployment, risk taking or pain and hurt!

Within this chapter, we have looked at selected statistics and trends that indicate both rapid external changes and internal difficulties in adjusting to these changes. Whether this is because of the particular external changes that young men are currently experiencing, or the particular mindset that some young men have, is, in part, the contents of the next chapter. What impact does masculinity have on the way that men respond to these external changes? How much is this as a result of being a man? And how much do we (as professional workers) need to understand about masculinity to enable us to intervene in young men's lives in a useful way? In short, can we attribute young men's reactions to changing circumstances and opportunities to the way they have been taught and have learnt about being a man?

References

1. Annual Abstract of Statistics 1993 HMSO.
2. Labour Force Survey Employment Department, GB, 1994.
3. Labour Force Survey CSO, 1995.
4. Harman, H. obtained from the Common's Library from unpublished Department of Employment data, 1995.
5. Charlton J. et. al. 'Suicide deaths in England and Wales: trends in factors associated with suicide deaths' Population Trends No 71, Spring 93, pp34-43.
6. Firn S. 'Peril of the stiff upper lip' Nursing Times 21st June 1995, Vol. 91, 23:60.
7. Gunnell D. and Frankel S. 'Prevention of suicide; aspirations and evidence' British Medical Journal 1994; 308.
8. Calman K. On the State of the Public Health HMSO, 1992.
9. Parents and Home Accident Prevention for Children under Five Health Promotion Agency for Northern Ireland, 1994.
10. Key Area Handbook on accidents, HMSO, 1991.
11. Kemble, B. 'Why Boys get Hurt and Girls Play Safe' Evening Standard 14th May 1993.
12. General Household Survey: Figures for Great Britain HMSO, 1995.
13. Home Office Statistical Bulletin 10/94.
12. Criminal Statistics England and Wales Government Statistical Service, 1994.
14. NAPO Report, August 1994.
15. Survey of young offenders reported at the Chief Police Officers' Annual Drugs Conference. Reported in The Independent 13th May 1993.
16. British Crime Survey Home Office, HMSO, 1993.
17. British Crime Survey Home Office, HMSO, 1994.
18. Criminal Statistics England and Wales Government Statistical Service, 1990.
19. Kilmartin CT. The Masculine Self MacMillan, New York, 1994.
20. Ruxton S. 'Boys Won't Be Boys: Tackling the Roots of Male Delinquency' in Lloyd T, and Wood T. (eds.) What Next for Men? Working With Men, London, 1996.
21. Equal Opportunities Commission. 1995
22. Sunday Times 19th June 1994.
23. Dept of Education and Employment Figures for England HMSO, 1996.
24. Department of Education figures and MORI poll of 79 local authorities, commissioned by Panorama in March 1993.
25. Lewis T. 'Unemployment and men's health' in Nursing vol 3 No 26, February 1988. M. Brenner. 'Mortality and the national economy' in The Lancet 1979, 2: pp568-9.

26. Skelton R. 'Man's role in society and its effect on health' in Nursing 26, vol 3, No. 26, February 1988. Wingard DL. 'The sex differential in morbidity, mortality and lifestyle'in Annual Review Public Health 1984, 5, pp433-58.

27. Baldings. J. Young People in 1992 Schools Health Education Unit, University of Exeter, 1993. Briscoe ME. 'Sex Differences in Mental Health' in Update 1st November 1989. pp834-839.

28. Rutter, M. and Smith D. Psychosocial Disorders in Young People: Time Trends and Their Causes Academia Europea, London, 1995.

29. Long VO. 'Relation of masculinity to self-esteem and self-acceptance in male professionals, college students, and scientists' in Journal of Counselling Psychology, 36: 84-87.

30. Haviland MG. et al. 'The relationship between alexithymia and depressive symtoms in a sample of newly alcoholic inpatients' in Psychotherapy and Psychosomatics 50: 81-87.

31. Derlega VJ. et al. Personality: contemporary theory and research Nelson Hall, Chicago, 1991.

32. Fitzgerald LF. & Cherpas CC. 'On the reciprocal relationship between gender and occupation: rethinking the assumptions concerning masculine career development' in Journal of Vocational Behaviour 27 : 109 122, 1985.

33. O'Neil JM. 'Assessing men's gender role conflict' in Moore D. and Leafgren F. (eds.) Men and Conflict (23-38) American Assoc. of Counselling and Development, Alexandria, VA., 1990.

34. Davis F. & Walsh WB. 'Antecedents and consequences of gender role conflict: an empirical test of sex role strain analysis' paper presented at the 96th Annual Convention of the APA, Atlanta, GA., 1988.

35. Kilmartin CT. The Masculine Self Macmillan, 1994.

36. Keele University, 1994.

37. Department of Education, 1993.

38. Hymas C. and Cohen J. 'The Trouble with Boys' in The Sunday Times 19th June 1994.

39. Strickland S. 'The Big Trouble with Boys' in The Independent 28th July 1994.

40. Mulgan G. and Wilkinson H. Freedom's Children DEMOS 1996.

Young men and masculinity

The foundations of work with boys should rest on an understanding of masculinity and its impact on young men. This is primarily what distinguishes it from good youthwork. Because of the centrality of masculinity, an understanding of what masculinity is, of how men learn about being men, of how men become men, and of what changes there have been in this process in the recent past, are all essential. This chapter, rather than being simply a trip through theoretical perspectives (see the resources list for this), reviews the issues and viewpoints that can assist practitioners to develop their work with boys and young men.

What is Masculinity?

An understanding of masculinity, unfortunately cannot be gained from the Oxford Dictionary. Masculinity has changed over the years, and our levels of understanding have grown enormously too. Like so many other attitudinal and behavioural concepts, masculinity can be understood within at least four broad theoretical frameworks: psychoanalysis, sociology, psychology and cultural studies have all contributed to our understanding of masculinity. These broad frameworks understand and/or stress different aspects of masculinity, and are often seen (by the writers at least) as being in conflict over the same territory. As practitioners, this 'one view' position seriously inhibits our ability to incorporate these often insightful understandings into our practice. This chapter therefore approaches the literature in terms of 'what is useful' to us as practitioners, and not what is 'correct'.

Masculinity and femininity are relatively recent concepts, and our understandings and concerns of both have changed and developed in the last 30 years. During the 60's, masculinity and femininity were seen on a single continuous dimension, with masculinity at one end and femininity at the other:

Masculinity   <·······································> Femininity

Attributes were assigned to one or other (so, for example, "Men are strong" and "Women are emotional") and scales were developed to find out where individuals were on this line. However, the distinction between masculinity and femininity was not seen as problematic in itself; individuals who found themselves at the 'wrong' end of the spectrum (women showing masculine characteristics, for example) were viewed as in need of help in developing sex appropriate characteristics. Some people will see unemployed men who are taking responsibility for their children and home (often while their wives are working), as 'wimpy' or in need of something to harden them up. This concept of individuals' inability to 'fit in the right hole' is now viewed as conservative in nature.

The 70's saw gender role theorists questioning this single, bipolar approach, developing instead the androgyny model that saw a healthy identity as a combination of both feminine and masculine characteristics[1]. Androgyny suggested that traditional masculinity (seen as high in masculine, and low in feminine, attributes) was in fact problematic, and this view certainly contributed to the questioning of sex role stereotyping and the move away from individuals being seen as needing to be taught and helped to develop 'appropriate' gender characteristics.

The 80's saw the development of the gender role strain model, which confirmed the problematic nature of masculinity and femininity raised by androgyny (and feminism), but went on to suggest that wider changes in society (employment trends, higher expectations of women and the absence of war) had made it increasingly difficult (and inappropriate) for men and women to take on the attributes and behaviours thought previously to be appropriate to them. Therefore, rather than seeing the individuals as inadequate in some way, the role strain model emphasised the mismatch between the individual and societal changes and expectations. Role strain advocates such as Pleck[2] stressed the damage that this process did on individual men as they tried to fit themselves into the male stereotype, and the mental health problems that being unemotional and trying to prove yourself a man could have on them. This view of masculinity has had most impact on the development of masculinity-based work with boys and young men.

How do we learn about being a man?

There are, predictably, a number of views about where men learn to be men. So, for example, biological psychologists believe that:

"Men are defined by their possession of a Y chromosome. Masculinity, they argue, follows as a consequence of this organic structure, particularly through the stimulation of the production of male sex hormones (androgens) which act directly upon the body's vital organs especially the brain. Masculinity does not so much 'get into' men as 'emerge out' of them"[3].

Most geneticists would, however, agree with Richard Lewontin[4] when he says:

"The primary self identification of a person as a man or a woman, with the multitude of attitudes, ideas, and desires that accompany that identification, depends on what label was attached to him or her as a child. In the normal course of events, these labels correspond to a consistent biological difference in chromosomes, hormones and morphology. Thus biological differences become a signal for, rather than a cause of, different social roles".

So, if we are biologically male, then the complex social interaction between ourselves and others will (in most cases) reinforce this biological fact. Most geneticists say we learn to be a man, but from where? Studies of mother infant interaction show differences in treatment of boys and girls (even medical personnel have been found to treat them differently). Hanson[5] found that new born males were often described as 'sturdy', 'handsome', or 'tough', while females were termed 'dainty', 'sweet', or 'charming', in spite of no differences in size or weight.

Early gender learning is thought to be unconscious, as both males and females speak, handle and treat boys and girls differently. By the age of two, children are thought to have a partial understanding of what gender is, knowing whether they are a 'boy' or a 'girl'. Toys, picture books and television have all been found to distinguish between males and females[6]. Books have been found to not only distinguish between males and females, but also to over represent boys. Lenore Weitzman [7] found that males played a much larger part in the stories and pictures than females, outnumbering them by a ratio of 11 to 1. When animals with gender identities were included, the ratio was 95 to 1, while male and female activities also differed.

By the time children start school, they are thought to have a clear consciousness of gender differences, and boys and girls are encouraged to concentrate on different activities and sports. Peer groups are also, of course, thought to play a major part in reinforcing and further shaping gender identity throughout a child's school career, with friendship circles, both in and out of school, often either all boy or all girl[6].

These studies are examples of gender learning, where boys and girls learn about what behaviours and attitudes they should have according to their label male or female. Gender identity is thought to be one of the most basic of self definitions.

While there is both agreement and substantial evidence that masculinity is (at least in part) learnt, how it is learnt, when it is learnt, and how much choice men have in what they learn are all open for debate. However, four perspectives dominate our current understandings of masculinity. Even the briefest description of these will be useful to contexturalise our understanding.

Psycho-analytical theorists assume some core psychological conflicts which men are thought to resolve in different ways to women. These conflicts are predictably thought to occur within boys' relationships with their mothers and fathers, and, for Freud, the central stage in the development of masculinity was 'the phallic or Oedipal stage'. Genital enquiry leads to sexual interest in his mother (assumed to be his main source of love, food and comfort) and rivalry with his father. Freud argued that boys have to learn to direct their attention away from their mothers to attain an 'appropriate genital heterosexuality'. He also argued that this phallic stage becomes symbolic for the boy's identity and, through fear of castration, he will identify with his father's power and internalise his father's voice (super ego).

While identification and introjection have remained important aspects of psychoanalysts' understandings of masculinity, more recent writers have been influenced by role theory and feminism. So, for example, Mitchell[8] questioned Freud's belief that gender identity was so closely associated with genital awareness and has questioned his apparent deduction that the penis is 'naturally' superior to the vagina. Mitchell also questioned Freud's belief that gender learning is concentrated in the Oedipal phase, believing (like many other authors) that learning occurs in infancy. Chodorow[9] has also suggested that the Oedipal transition occurs differently for boys and girls (who remain close to their mothers), and that boys gain a sense of self via a more radical rejection of their closeness to their mothers, forging their understanding of masculinity from what is not feminine. They have to learn not to be 'cissies'. As a result, Chodorow suggests, boys are relatively unskilled in relating closely to others, and develop more analytical ways of looking at the world.

The other problem with Freud's analysis is, of course, that he implies the normality of a heterosexual identity, that this is, by definition, the only desirable sexual preference.

It is difficult to see how these relationships and sometimes unconscious drives and issues can assist us as practitioners, outside of a psychotherapeutic environment! Some practitioners have attempted to incorporate this within their work with men (see [10], for example), but the gulf between theory and practice appears to be immense.

A more useful conceptual framework for practitioners has been the identification by role theorists of a set of 'social scripts' (such as the need for soldiers to defend society) that individuals are then tailored to fit.

"Masculine roles involve a set of expectations for task orientated behaviours that emphasise logic and rationality and de emphasise emotional experience. From early childhood, boys come to value masculine traits and behaviours and devalue feminine ones"[11].

Gender role theory is concerned with dissecting components of masculinity, dividing these into self and others. Within the self concept, we have "how I am as a man", and the ideal self concept "how I should be as a man" and "how I should not be as a man". Within the others, we have stereotypes of "how men are", and norms — "how men should be" and "how men should not be"[11].

Role theorists are concerned about the way that individuals manage to, and fail to, make these different components match up to each other. These concerns are shared by the practitioner; the questions themselves are attractive as the basis for discussion with young men, and the tensions between the self and others provide further discussion material.

The social relations perspective sees masculinity as a set of distinctive practices which take their shape from social structures. Men are moulded by their inter-relationship with these structures. One of the main differences between gender role theory and the social relations perspective have been highlighted by writers such as Connell[12], who has questioned the inevitability of gender role theory (which suggests that men will learn what they are told passively). Connell argues that this interplay between men and the social structures is also about benefits and gains that individual men may get by accepting these roles, and, in some cases, striving for the status and power that accompanies them. The social relations perspective leans heavily on gender role theory as the means of learning to be a man, although it contributes a lot to discussions about motivation and the inter-related nature of masculinity, femininity and power.

Of all the broad perspectives on how we learn to be a man, the social relations perspective offers us the most. It expands the role strain model (about the interrelated nature of the individual and their social setting); offers a view of individuals' ability to choose and to take responsibility about what they learn; and distinguishes between gender-based models (reflecting differences between masculinity and femininity), as well as sexism-based models (reflecting institutional and individual power imbalances).

The cultural perspective suggests that masculinity is transmitted from one generation to the next, although again the suggestion is that this is learnt and that it consists of individuals' perception of themselves, as well as of society and others. This perspective leans heavily on an understanding of culture that is *"passed down from generation to generation, through which ordinary people conduct and make sense of their everyday lives"*[3].

Cultural codes, visual images, historical changes and ideology are important to this perspective, and learning is thought to be through observation, others' actions, conscious and unconscious understandings, and recognition of "recycled culture"[3]. Within this perspective, writers such as Gilmore [13] see masculinity as a direct response to particular social and environmental conditions. He details a number of examples of situations where men are 'encouraged' to exhibit masculine qualities for their own (and others') survival. Alternatively, Hoch[14] has posited that society swings between two different reflections of masculinity. He suggests that, in times of economic hardships, the Puritan view of masculinity (hard work and physical toughness) is strongest, while, in times of improved economic conditions, a defined and exclusive wealthy and leisure-orientated masculinity separates a small, powerful group of men from others. Both Gilmore and Hoch draw from popular culture, fashion, media images, ritual and popularist understandings of what masculinity is.

The cultural perspective has had its influence on practitioners, as it provides a model of attitudes and beliefs that are often separate from the social context of many young men. For instance, even when they are third generation unemployed, and therefore have not been given 'role model' experience, young men can still hold very strong beliefs, such as "Men are bread-winners".

The fourth, and last, perspective worthy of mention is feminism, where masculinity is viewed as a set of power relations where men assert power given to them via their gender to maximise material and self-esteem rewards. Until recently, many feminists viewed "all men as monolithic oppressors of women"[15]. More recently, writers have suggested that there are "two hierarchical systems male domination of women and the inter male dominance hierarchies, where groups of men have different levels of power"[16].

It is difficult to imagine the interest there now is in work with boys without the feminist perspective. Feminism initiated the widespread discussion about gender in the 60's and 70's, and girlswork forced a debate and response from men about gender work in youthwork.

Most of the readers of this book will see their own views about masculinity reflected within this chapter. There are some similarities between all of the perspectives, in that they identify external people, roles or institutions that teach, offer rewards and sometimes force men into a masculine way of being.

Some authors have highlighted important themes that have changed the way we view masculinity. So, for instance, Brittan and others have argued that:

"masculinity refers to those aspects of men's behaviour that fluctuate over time. In some cases, these fluctuations may last for decades in others, it may be a matter of weeks or months"[17].

Masculinity changes and adapts to the social context and the nature of what men learn about being a man can, and does, alter it is not a set series of attributes that have been constant for hundreds of years. However, Brittan also suggests that there is a more rigid construction running parallel with these sometimes fast-changing masculinities: he calls this masculinism and sees this as:

"the ideology that justifies and naturalises male domination. As such it is the ideology of patriarchy; masculinism takes it for granted that there is a fundamental difference between men and women, it assumes that heterosexuality is normal, it accepts without question the sexual division of labour, and it sanctions the political and dominant role of men in the public and private spheres"[17].

Some of us may refer to this as a 'traditional masculinity'. This distinction is helpful as it suggests that, while a rigid view of 'being a man' influences the learning process, it will often overlap and sometimes be in conflict with a changing and adapting number of masculinities. So, for example, while the traditional view stresses that men are breadwinners and women are carers of children and their responsibilities lie in these separate departments, external factors such as the rapidly changing employment trends are impacting on both masculinity and femininity. Individual men can grow up with both of these images impacting on their attitudes and behaviours.

Connell [12 & 15] and others have also stressed the importance of identifying a number of masculinities, rather than a single masculinity. While Connell highlights a hegomonic masculinity (similar to Brittan's masculinism and the 'traditional view'), he also stresses the influences that class, race, sexuality, disability and other identity and social factors have on 'what being a man is' for different men. So, for African-Caribbean men, the images they have of being a man will be different from Irish men.

For those of us that work with men, these distinctions between a fixed traditional view, and the development of new and changing images of masculinity are very important to keep in mind. So is the importance of recognising that different groups of men are likely to have different constructions of masculinity impacting on their lives as well as the more traditional view.

When do we become men?

We have looked above at the process of learning to become a man, but when does it actually happen? Work with Boys [18] focused on the basic contradiction between being young and male.

The contradiction

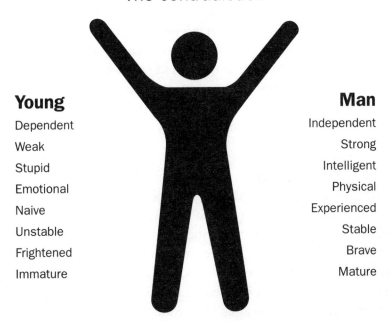

Young	**Man**
Dependent	Independent
Weak	Strong
Stupid	Intelligent
Emotional	Physical
Naive	Experienced
Unstable	Stable
Frightened	Brave
Immature	Mature

Over the last 10 years, within training courses, this picture of the process has rung bells for practitioners about both their own lives and those of the young men they work with.

The basic premise is that young men are given two contradictory views of who they are. On the one hand they are told that they are Young (and therefore weak and dependent), while on the other they are told that they are Male (and therefore strong and independent). Because social value is given to the Male characteristics, then this basic contradiction between being Young and Male leads young men to 'prove' that they are Male and not Young. This model is based on a number of key assumptions about when, and how, we learn about masculinity and being a man.

The first assumption is that there is, in fact, a transition, that the gulf between childhood and adulthood (reflected in the two lists of characteristics) requires individuals to move from one to the other – from being Young to being a Man. This transition is comparatively recent: only since industrialisation has childhood been given a separate status from adulthood. While our notions of pre-industrial life are often romantic, children were seen then as small people who grew up and learnt what there was to learn, but who were fundamentally inexperienced and weaker adults, and not a completely separate species.

With fine pieces of legislation, such as the Education and the Factories Acts, ensuring that young people were given a formal education and avoided workplace exploitation, came confirmation of a difference between being a child and an adult. Zelizer[19] has described a transition "from an economically useful to the economically useless childhood" as a gradual and uneven process, "vehemently supported by reformers, but resisted with equal conviction by working class and middle class advocates of a productive childhood. It was partly a matter of conflicting economic interest, but mostly an ideological dispute between two opposing views of childhood".

Of course, the separation was further ideologically confirmed by the 'discovery' of adolescence. As the gap between childhood and adulthood grew, something had to fill the void. Coleman and Hendry[20] have suggested that:

"there is now a preference for viewing adolescence as a transitional process rather than as a stage or number of stages. To conceptualise the period in this way implies that adolescence needs to be understood as a time during which the individual passes from one state childhood to another maturity and that the issues and problems faced by individuals during this period are predominantly the result of the transitional process".

They go on to say:

"This transition, it is believed, results from the operation of a number of pressures. Some of these, in particular the physiological

and emotional pressures, are internal, while other pressures which originate from peers, parents, teachers, and society at large, are external to the young person".

It is within this context that this transition between being Young and Male needs to be understood. These stages of life are socially constructed and have continued to make the transition between being a boy and a man difficult. Bly [21] has suggested that we have 'lost' transitional points and offers endless examples of non-industrialised societies that have events that mark the move from boyhood to manhood. Acts of bravery, demands of courage, the ability to be independent and self-sufficient, are all reflected within these transitional points. Bly is quite right to highlight the loss of these, but either fails to understand, or chooses to ignore, the changing social context of them. The separation of children from the economic process in the 19th Century created a gap, which has now become a chasm, between childhood and adulthood.

Two aspects seem to be central to the nature of this transition, firstly the literal 'gap' between childhood and adulthood, and secondly, the ease with which individuals can move from one to the other.

Even as recently as the early 60's, the future for most young men was relatively predictable, even though the distinction between being a child and an adult was confirmed. Jobs were relatively plentiful (unemployment was at 1.5%, and even lower for young men) and 74.6% of 15-19 year-olds (school leaving age was 15), were economically active [22]. Most young men knew that, even if they were trapped in childhood, when they arrived at 15, they could leave school, get a job, and earn money, and, for many, the transition from being Young to Male was eventful, but inevitable and relatively short-lived. The nature of 'proving' yourself a man hinged around role activity. 'Becoming' a worker, a husband and father confirmed (for heterosexual men at least) manhood.

In comparison, current male unemployment for young

men under 20 years is 12.5%; a total of 35.4% are econo-mically inactive, with only 51.2% in full-time work. 34% of 16-19-year-old males who are unemployed have been out of work for more than 13 weeks[23], while, in 1989, 69% of 16-18-year-olds were still in education or training.

On this evidence alone, the gap between childhood and adulthood (assuming that work remains one of the main transition points), has both grown and become much more difficult to cross, for young men in particular. Added to this is the reduction in numbers of young men who are heads of households[24] and married or living with a partner.

The second assumption is that this transition process has internal and external aspects, both of which put a strain on individual young men. We are much more aware of the external aspects (such as employment rates, risk-taking behaviours and violence, etc.) than we are of the internal. To date, we have less evidence of what goes on in young men's minds and, indeed, their hearts.

Historically, this transition period has had a form of social contract between society and young men. Society has promised young men an important role (usually as soldiers or workers) if they are prepared to wait, make at least some effort at school and stay within the law. Society has also been prepared to accept a certain amount of "boys being boys" and having a bit of fun. When the transition period was relatively short (as recently as the early 60's, 15 was the school leaving age), then adolescence was hardly a blink. Other transitional sites such as alcohol, drugs, sport, girls, sexuality and puberty were still preoccupations for parents and society, but these operated within a strong role-driven agreement. Even those that fell outside of school and the law could be rehabilitated and put back into adult, male roles. Young offenders, and those that truanted or left school as 'failures', were still able to make the transition.

Of course, now, not only have the role opportunities reduced substantially, but housing opportunities, the school leaving age (while legally being 16, for the majority it has risen to 18) and adolescence have extended the transition period from 3-4 years to more like 10-14 years. A blink has become a decade or more, and, for many, the social contract has collapsed. Young men's willingness to wait has disappeared along with the clearly-defined social role previously offered to them by society. This lack of 'stakeholding', as Blair has called it, is, of course, impacting on other groups apart from young men, but the importance of this for young men is that (as young people) they have started outside the stakeholding society and have tended to need to be brought into it. Dench[25] has used the story of the Frog Prince to reflect the state of the male. He suggests that it is not unusual to symbolise men as animals; that this reflects the wildness and the inhuman, and, in the form of the frog, the mess and the vulnerability. The frog is destined to live this life in the wilderness until the princess offers to make him human and enable him to live in the comforts of society. Dench stresses the importance of this transition from 'wildness' to within society's structures.

While, for many, the social contract has collapsed, the need to make this transition has not. With the loss of transition into work and independence, some of what were previously secondary sites have taken on an added importance. Alcohol abuse, mindless violence, "road rage" (as we now call mindless violence somewhere near a car or road), and general levels of risk-taking behaviour have all taken on a more significant role in many men's lives. Or the opposite has occurred, with young men withdrawing from the "proving environments", giving up, and turning to drugs for solace, or to suicide for relief.

Unless we address the lack of transition points, the significant changes and the collapsing social contract between young men and society, significant numbers of young men will return to the Dench woods, if not in the image of the film Lord of the Flies, then at least in their minds. Substantial groups of young African-Caribbean and working class white young men are already there; others will follow.

For some, the answer is simple – create enough jobs for these young men to step into, value them in the traditional way, reintroduce the social contract. The problem with this is that the employment trends are not moving towards traditional male jobs, which are well-paid, but towards lower-paid service jobs perceived by many (men and women) as 'women's jobs'. The economy is moving away from the traditional male workplace. For others, the solution is equally simple – we re-introduce transitional points for young men to pass through, enabling young men to take on the male adult role. While Bly [21] and others have been wrongly ridiculed for their suggestion that we have lost these transitional points and need to reintroduce them, the social context of these transitional rituals have always relied upon a clearly-defined role for the 'new men'. Transitional rituals only have value if indeed they are transitional points into a social context. Bly and others have wrongly suggested that ritual acceptance into a society of men is enough, when, in fact, the impact of transitional points are internal (on the individual), external (on the society of men) and also social (within the context of a clearly-defined role). Without this social context, transitional points have only a limited appeal and impact.

This is not to deny the value that many men seemed to have gained by returning to the open air and 'acting out' these rituals, but the gains are therapeutic in nature, not social in value. For some men, in hindsight, there will be a value in returning to this part of their lives, but for young men without a clear social context, the experience will be hollow.

The Scout movement provides an interesting example of ritual transition for boys and young men. Born out of a view that the country's young men were not strong, fit and, indeed, fed enough to ensure a healthy army, the Scout movement provided a series of transitional points that boys could mark as they moved towards manhood. However, without the overarching social purpose of strengthening the army, the Scouts would have been, at best, boys playing soldiers and learning a series of skills that would help them to survive.

The transition from boyhood to manhood does have enormous significance and bearing on many young men's need to prove that they are men, levels of risk-taking and self-esteem. While it is obviously not the only factor to consider in young men's lives, transition and becoming a man (especially as the social circumstances are changing so rapidly) are increasingly more significant and important isues for workers of all professions coming into contact with young men to raise and address.

This chapter has aimed to review the perspectives that have some direct impact on working with boys and young men, to help to think about the aspects of theory that we may be able to draw on in our developing practice. A list of useful theoretically-based books can be found in the 'resources and further reading' section.

References

1. Bem S. 'The Measurement of Psychological Androgyny' in Journal of Consulting and Clinical Psychology 42, 155-162.
2. Pleck J. The Myth of Masculinity MIT Press, Cambridge, MA., 1981.
3. Edley N and Wetherell M. Men in Perspective (Practice, Power and Identity) Prentice Hall, London, 1995.
4. Lewontin R. Human Diversity. Freeman, London, 1982.
5. Hanson J. 'Sex education for young children' in Scanzoni J. & Fox GL. Sex Role Family and Society (Journal of Marriage and the Family 42).
6. Giddens A. Sociology Polity Press, Cambridge, 1993.
7. Weitzman L. 'Sexual socialization in picture books for preschool children' in American Journal of Sociology 77: 1972.
8. Mitchell J. Psychoanalysis and feminism Allen Lane, London, 1974.

9. Chodorow N. The Reproduction of Mothering: Psychoanalysis and the Sociology of Gender University of California Press, Berkeley, 1978.

10. Jukes A. Why Men Hate Women Free Association Books, Salisbury, 1993.

11. Kilmartin CT. The masculine self MacMillan, New York, 1994.

12. Connell RW. Masculinities Polity, Cambridge, 1995.

13. Gilmore DD. Manhood in the making: Cultural concepts of masculinity Yale University Press, London, 1990.

14. Hoch P. White hero, black beast: Racism, sexism and the mask of masculinity Pluto Press, London, 1979.

15. Connell RW. Gender & Power Polity, Cambridge, 1987.

16. Sabo D. & Gordon DF. Men's Health and Illness (Gender, power, and the body) Sage, London, 1995.

17. Brittan A. Masculinity and power Blackwell, Oxford, 1989.

18. Lloyd T. Work With Boys NYB, Leicester, 1985.

19. Zelizer VA. Pricing the Priceless Child Basic Books New York 1985.

20. Coleman JC. & Hendry L. The nature of adolescence Routledge, London, 1990.

21. Bly R. Iron John: A Book About Men Element Books, 1991.

22. The Annual Abstracts HMSO, 1976.

23. OPCS HMSO, 1991.

24. Social Trends HMSO, 1996.

25. Dench G. The Frog The Prince & The Problem of Men Neanderthal Books, London, 1994.

Understanding into practice

Having looked at the current statistics and at masculinity, we need to identify what these might mean for young men and our own developing practice.

Currently, a lot of individuals and agencies are talking about young men as a 'problem'. Crime, school underachievement, drug and alcohol abuse, violence and suicide are all recurrent discussion themes. Young men are in our thoughts, but usually problematised.

To date, we have too often responded to these problems and issues in predictable ways. We have blamed young men for their behaviour; for not being mature enough; for not taking the opportunities provided for them. Head teachers may say, "School is there to teach – if they want to disrupt it, then we will deal with that disruption". We have too often put the problem down to the young men's lack of certain characteristics and attributes: "If only young men could talk about how they feel, they wouldn't commit suicide". Some have blamed society for not providing enough opportunities: "If there were more jobs, young men would not thieve, and crime figures would come down - it is the Government's fault". Fault and blame have too frequently been a poor substitute for dealing with a complex set of issues and problems.

We need, initially, to acknowledge what is happening. The statistics in Chapter Two reflect a worrying picture. They are not a series of unconnected data, but an overall trend that suggests that the situation for young men is critical and in need of understanding and intervention. Attempts to allocate blame tend to perpetuate inactivity; without action and understanding, this is one problem that is unlikely to go away.

One hindrance (and, in fact, this is all it can be) is our collective uncertainty about whether gender is, in fact, inherent. What if it is natural for young men to be violent? What if testosterone makes young men think the way they do? For many of us, biological explanations are a nagging worry, particularly in terms of young men's ability to change, and indeed, our ability to intervene effectively. There are enough indicators to suggest that biology does have an impact, but to what degree we don't (and probably will never) know. We also have enough indications to suggest that socialisation has a major impact; and this is surely enough to indicate that appropriate intervention can, and will, have good effect.

Another barrier is what Michael Kimmel has called "the silence of masculinity" [1]. He suggests that, while we know a lot about women and femininity, masculinity is rarely acknowledged, let alone addressed. One of the common links between many of the statistics in Chapter Two is masculinity. Unless we acknowledge this and look at its implications on our strategic planning and practice, we are unlikely to get much further than blame and silence.

Another hindrance for action is the view that we need to know more about young men; that research needs to be the cutting edge; that, at some stage, we think we will know enough, and appropriate strategies will then become obvious. This will never happen, we will never know enough, and, indeed, whether strategic planning can, and should, be research-led is open to question. The rapidly-changing social circumstances that young men find themselves in suggest that we know enough to develop an intervention-focused strategy. Research is important, but surely on the basis of 'need to know'. Maybe the question we have to ask is, "What do we need to know about young men, to enable us to develop practice and policy?".

Having said that, to a large extent, young men are still relatively unknown. Current literature has looked at their behaviour [2], their views about aspects of their lives [3], and the changing circumstances they find themselves in. However, how much do we know about them? What do they think about their current circumstances, and how do they feel about them? Recent publications such as Aggleton [4] and Harland [5] are a rarity: researchers providing young men with an environment where they can talk about what they think and feel are rare, but essential if we are really to find out about young men, their needs and aspirations.

Probably, understanding what we know is more important than more data and research. Understanding the changing relationship between masculinity, the social circumstances young men find themselves in, and the impact and affect these have on young men themselves, is essential. This will continue to be an important, complex series of relationships for us to grapple with.

What we certainly need are bold workers with a vision, abilities and skills, including the ability to support and help our young men to develop the skills and attributes they themselves will need in the next millennium. Workers who are able and willing to engage with young men, to help them adapt to their rapidly-changing circumstances. Without these workers, it is difficult to see where young men will find help to adapt. Of course, masculinity has always changed and men have adapted to these changes. However, how well men do, and can, adapt, how much fall-out there is for individual men, and how deep the impact is on society, can be influenced by policy and practice.

To enable workers to be bold and develop their skills, they need to be encouraged to experiment, try different approaches and engage very actively with young men. Management in schools, youth services and criminal justice settings, seems to be moving towards caution and conservatism through, in part, the need for cuts and an economically-led view of 'value for money'. These all mitigate against experimentation. However, unless workers are supported, they are unlikely to feel able to develop the skills they will need to address the current issues.

We need to engage with young men about the real issues that are affecting them. For example, within the statistics of young men's underachievement at school, there are a substantial number of young men who feel that they have been let down by society, particularly in terms of jobs and a role for themselves as men: up until recently, there has always been a clear-cut role as a worker, or, indeed, soldier. This must have an impact on young men's aspirations, their self-perception and their security about who they are. It is no surprise that an increasing number of young men are become disaffected and giving up at school. These and other issues affecting young men can't be ignored.

We have to develop and record effective ways of working with young men, teasing out what is transferable, what can be duplicated and what young men will respond to.

We have to understand much more about how people generally change and how young men, in particular, change. What works in terms of helping young men change their attitudes, beliefs and behaviours? So often, we talk about established beliefs about manhood, relationships with women, men's roles and sexism. These are not usually changed by leaflets or a short chat! The more we understand how attitudes and beliefs can be changed, the more we can understand the task we are engaged in.

We need to enable the exploration and reflection on these attitudes and beliefs wherever we can. When workers discuss where this should happen, many suggest the school curriculum, and argue that it belongs next to maths and science, life skills and an understanding of the world we live in. This is, of course, true, but it does ignore the piling up of subject matter within the current curriculum, and risks ignoring the other possible environments where young men may be receptive, indeed even more receptive. Youth clubs, careers, other training environments, the family, are all settings where young men can be encouraged to think about the changing nature of their world.

One of the very noticeable losses over the last two decades has been the series of 'safety nets' that people could use-extended families, pastoral teachers, agencies that catered for different groups of people at different levels of crisis. In some areas, the number of services to engage between a small worry and the Samaritans can be very few, especially if you are a member of a group that has traditionally been reluctant to use services. We need to develop services that target young men (this doesn't mean just organising around sport and activity) and find as many different routes as possible for young men to receive help and have opportunities to think, feel, reflect and make decisions about their lives and relationships.

There are also a number of skills that masculinity seems to leave many young men lacking. Adaptability and flexibility are obvious ones, but there is also a series of skills and abilities associated with parenthood (such as the ability to recognise feelings and knowing how to respond to them) that will hinder many men's ability, confidence and probable interest in becoming more active in childcare and fatherhood in particular.

We need to think through the impact of masculinity on what men are likely to learn, believe and think about themselves and others. However, we also need to acknowledge that there are probably more differences between men than similarities, and therefore we must be very reluctant to make too many assumptions about 'men in general'. Any statement that begins, "All men are.....", is more likely to be a stereotype than a statement of fact. Assumptions are there to be tested – "Do all the young men I know act in the same way?". Asking the question helps us tease out fact from fiction, assumptions from facts, ensuring that our knowledge base is just that, and not a mixture of half-truths.

This section has concentrated on understanding and aspects that need to be in place to enable the development of practice. Part Two of this book concentrates on what we can do, but certainly assumes that, without bold and skilled workers, we are unlikely to have developing practice, and, without straightforward policies (that primarily support practice), we will have little coherent and consistent practice.

References

1. Kimmel M. 'Try Supporting Feminism!' in Lloyd T. and Wood T. What Next for Men? Working With Men, London, 1996.
2. Willis P. Learning to Labour.
3. Turkie A. What do you Mean? National Youth Bureau, Leicester, 1986.
4. Aggleton P. et. al. Young Men Speak Out. Health Education Authority, London, 1995.
5. Harland K. Young Men Talking (Voices from Belfast) Working With Men, London, 1997.

Part Two
Addressing the Issues

Developing practice

At the most fundamental level, we have two problems – one is that many young men have difficulties in communicating and expressing themselves, while the second is that many professional workers have difficulties in developing their relationships and work with young men.

Unfortunately, too many professional workers have tended to externalise 'the problem' as being the young men's. Indeed, it has not only been professional workers that have concluded that young men are the problem. Whether it was governmental concern at the turn of the century that young men were not strong enough to fight wars (provoking the creation of the Scouts); the media's panic in the 60's that 'mods' and 'rockers' were a reflection of young men being out of control (bringing about Abermarle and youth services as we now know them); or our current concerns that more and more young men are becoming lawless and without morals, our response to young men has too often been to see them as a problem.

If we are to assist young men to address some of the difficulties they have, we will have to go further than to 'just' externalise the problem. Acknowledging the difficulties we ourselves have in building relationships and developing our work with young men is a very important first step.

In Part One of this book, we looked at the nature of masculinity; now is the time to look at some of the implications this has on our work with young men. How does the process of growing up male (and the need to prove this), impact on young men's lives? What qualities, attributes, beliefs and difficulties does it leave young men with? As discussed in Part One, because of the competing nature of masculinities, statements that start with "all men", or even "most men", are very difficult to evidence. However, there are a number of attributes, behaviours and ways of thinking that do impact on substantial numbers of young men, and are important considerations for those of us developing work with them.

Recognition of feelings

Many young men, when asked "What do you feel?", will answer "Nothing", or "I don't know". When responses are encouraged, they describe this as being less about whether they really feel something and more as a difficulty in describing what they feel. This difficulty in 'recognising feelings' would appear, at least in part, to be as a result of a narrowing down of the 'types' of feelings young men are able to exhibit and those they are discouraged and encouraged to feel as appropriate to their gender assignment.

The most obvious of these is, of course, "Big boys don't cry". 'Big' in this respect seems to mean 7 years-of-age. Parents, teachers and other adults (often out of concern for how such boys will be treated) discourage their sons, pupils and boys they know from crying. Parents will often say they "don't want him to be bullied, and picked on because he cries"; teachers may say, "Don't let them see you cry, or they will pick on you more". Our motivation may be one of protection, however the message to these boys is "Don't cry". Most boys learn not to cry before they are seven. Other feelings and emotions, such as love, caring, fear, grief and hurt, are all discouraged and/or stopped, leaving boys finding it difficult to acknowledge, or, indeed, recognise, much of what they are feeling.

Talking about feelings

While many young men appear to have difficulties in

recognising their feelings, they often also have difficulties in talking about them (whether they recognise them or not). Related to this is the way that many young men receive and internalise the message that talking about their feelings is wrong, inappropriate and not welcomed by others. Professional workers will often describe situations where young men are encouraged to talk about themselves and how they feel, and they don't, or won't – they are resistant, or reluctant; they will leave, change the subject, look at their shoes, or make light or fun of it.

Lacking essential skills

The nature of growing up male seems to discourage the development of certain skills and attributes, notably adaptability and flexibility. Employers and teachers often talk about the difficulties (or reluctance) of young men to show flexibility towards their education, or towards their futures. Often, two groups of young men are described. The first are those that think they will play striker for Manchester United, or believe that, irrespective of the changing job market, there will be a good job out there for them (although they will probably have to wait). The second group are those young men who appear to have given up on their futures, living for the day or accepting that their futures may be outside of the mainstream. Research has reflected an adaptability in many young women, who are prepared to sacrifice enjoyment for now if they reap benefits later (girls will stay in, and do their homework, while many boys are more reluctant to do their homework, thinking that school work will be easy, that they will succeed without really trying, and that they will be seen in a poor light by their mates).

This would appear to occur, at least in part, because of the historical relationship that men have had with work. Even minimal effort by them at school has usually led to work, while women have always moved in and out of the employment market, in and out of childcare and domestic responsibilities, thus developing higher levels of adaptability and flexibility.

In the current employment market (and, indeed, life generally), these skills are essential, and not just desirable; without them, boys are at a clear disadvantage.

Behavioural problems

A number of the statistics highlighted earlier reflect a series of behavioural problems that are gender related. Gilmartin[1], when looking at sex differences in mental disorders, shows that:

1 Males experience a disproportionate number of many childhood disorders, for example, attention deficit hyperactivity disorder and conduct disorder.

2 Women are much more likely to have an eating disorder and somewhat more likely to be diagnosed with depression and most anxiety-based disorders.

3 Males constitute a majority of substance abusers, sexual deviates, and people with behaviour-control problems such as pyromania, compulsive gambling, and angry outbursts.

4 There are unequal sex proportions for a variety of personality disorders: more men than women are diagnosed as paranoid (67%), antisocial (82%), narcissistic (70%), and schizoid (78%); while more women than men are diagnosed as histrionic (85%), 'borderline' (62%), and dependent (69%).

5 Men are much more likely that women to commit suicide, although women make more 'unsuccessful' suicide attempts'.

These factors are obviously reflected in the amount of young men disaffected, truanting and involved in school behavioural 'incidents', and the proportions of young men in behavioural units, young offender institutions and other projects that deal with anti-social behaviour.

The social contract and young men

Less that 30 years ago, the social contract between young men and society was that, if young men stayed within the law and tried at school (even if they left without qualifications), then a job would be their reward. Society has broken this unspoken agreement, and this has provoked many young men to say, "Why bother at school?", or "It doesn't matter how hard you try, you get nothing". Work remains central to many men's view of what it is to be a man. The loss of this agreement has to be displaced somewhere, and must contribute to some of young men's need to prove that they are men.

Workers and young men

Having looked at some of the difficulties than young men have as a result of growing up male, we need to now address some of the issues that professionals encounter in their work with young men. In many respects, they are similar (or result from) the difficulties that young men have.

In a series of interviews with youth workers, the comments made about working with young men included:

"Young men only want to do sports and activities; they don't want to sit and talk";

"Holding their concentration for discussion is difficult";

"I would like to develop and improve my communication skills with young men, to enable me to offer formal/informal discussion groups, and also deal with disruptive elements with such groups"[2].

Young men's and professional workers' difficulties are often the same! Many young men find expressing and recognising their feelings hard: workers, in turn, find it difficult to generate discussion, hold attention and enable young men to talk openly - this is particularly the case for male workers.

Young men will often reflect their difficulties in talking about how they feel through disruptive or inappropriate behaviour. Workers find this difficult to deal with, but are also distracted from the difficulty, too often responding only to the disruptive behaviour. This often leads professionals working closely with young men to describe young men in problem terms. A young man can become a series of negative adjectives ("He is disruptive, rude, unable to concentrate; frankly, he is a pain. I am fed up with him in my class"). However true this may be of aspects of his behaviour and attitude, however much it may appear so, this is not all there is to him! Unless we acknowledge this tendency, we can become locked into behaving and responding to the young men's disruptive behaviour, and look less and less at ways we could respond and intervene differently, leading in turn to a loss of confidence.

Professional workers will often describe young men as a group, or a pack, in that their descriptions of young men are often confined to the 'group behaviour' they exhibit. Again, descriptions of their disruption dominate. Rarely do you hear of the young men's individual likes, passions, skills and qualities – too often their problematic nature is at the forefront of the professional worker's mind. This unbalanced view of young men leads to a definition of the problem as being the young men themselves. Workers all too easily externalise the problem and do what they so often accuse the young men of doing – refuse to take responsibility for the situation they find themselves in, namely, of having to deal with individual (and groups of) young men, experiencing difficulties and feeling fearful, or reluctant, to address them.

Parallel with these issues are a series of 'practice tensions' that many workers struggle with. Most of these come from a clash between ideology and practice. They include:

1 Whether the focus of work is primarily young men or others. Do we approach gender or sexism, do we do work because of young men's needs or because of the impact young men may have on others (e.g. violence)?

2 Do we start with process or outcomes? Sometimes, when Working With Men are asked to carry out work with young men, we are asked to "run a young men's group". We respond by asking why a young men's group has been proposed, and often find that workers are much clearer about method or style (such as single-sex environments) than they are about purpose and aims.

3 Ideology often interferes with our approaches to young men, especially if it dovetails with an emphasis on the negative aspects of young men's behaviour.

4 An understanding of sexism often leads many workers to look at young men 'through' this ideology. They will look at young men and see only a sexist jumble of behaviours and attitudes, and nothing else. Or some workers will look at young men and take the "boys will be boys" viewpoint, and say, "They don't really mean it", "They will grow out of it", or, indeed, "They will be fine when they meet the right young woman". These positions stop us from seeing young men as more rounded, complex people.

Steps to developing practice

Having reviewed masculinity, its impact on young men, and the difficulties that arise within the development of practice for both young men and professional workers, it is time to address the development of practice itself.

Over the last 14 years, those of us at Working With Men and The B Team have been developing work with young men. We have run courses/sessions in schools, youth clubs, criminal justice settings, colleges and other environments where young men go. On the back of that practice, we have also run training courses for teachers, youth workers, probation workers and health service personnel, looking at ways that their work with young men could be developed.

In spite of this extensive experience, we have found the reproduction of practice to be much more complex than simply suggesting to workers that they go off and do what we do. We have found that workers seem more able to develop practice on the basis of their own approaches and strengths, coupled with a greater understanding of some of the underpinning principles that have developed from our practice. This section will therefore concentrate on those underlying principles and elements of practice that have developed out of an understanding of how masculinity impacts on young men's lives.

But first some initial questions to consider:

What is your general motivation for working with young men?
Motivations range from wanting to meet the needs of young men; to wanting to stop their sexism; to being annoyed because of the way we were bullied or hurt as young men; to wanting to sort them out because they are so disruptive in the youth club or to make them 'nicer' human beings. Clarity about our motivation is essential if we are to work effectively.

Why do you want to work with young men at this point?
This may be influenced by your motivation, but may also be because your manager says you have to, or because they are currently being difficult or disruptive. Again, clarity of why you want to work with them will help you work effectively.

What do you like about them individually?
Considering this question will enable you to gauge how much

you know the young men. Do you know what they like? What they care about? Who they are (outside of the setting you see them in)? What do you already know about them? What more do you need to know about them? And, finally, what do you like about them?

What else do you like about them individually?
Indulge me. The more you know, and the more you can see their strengths and what you like, the more you are likely to work effectively with the young men.

How does their uncertainty about being men affect them individually and as a group?
How do they prove themselves? How much of the time you are with them are they able to relax and 'be themselves'? How do they wind each other up? How do they play on each other's uncertainty about being men?

What difficulties will arise for you working with these young men? Where do you feel uncertain about yourself, and where do you feel confident?
Are you nervous with them? Do they scare you? Have you known them long enough to have strong relationships? Have they been used to a relationship built on activity, with you helping them, or on sitting and chatting? How will this impact on and affect the work you are planning to do with them?

What is your current relationship with these young men, and how might that impact on your work with them?
Be very honest and realistic with yourself.

Practice Principles
Having considered these questions, it is time to think about what constitutes the work. Set out below is a series of underlying principles. These constitute some of the common

themes that are prominent within current developing practice. Their purpose is to help you think through your work with young men. Some may have wider use, some may not ring true within your way of working, while others may be right on the button. They are not intended as practice rules, but underlying principles that help you reflect on, and develop, your own practice.

1. Clarity of purpose, aims and outcomes

Clarity about why you are doing what you are doing, what you are doing, and how you are going to do it, is essential. So often within this area of work, the need is voiced for 'a boys group' (in the same way as girlswork was too often seen as a girls group) without a clarity of purpose. The method of transport needs to be determined by the destination and length of the journey, not the other way around. However, too often this is what we do when setting up work with young men. Purpose must determine everything else, followed by aims and outcomes and then method, form and style. So for example:

The purpose -the numbers of suicides for young men are on the increase, and, through a needs assessment, it is apparent that young men are unaware of services available to them in this area; they lack the confidence to make use of these services and are unsure about how they will be perceived by others, if they were to use these services. The purpose of this project is to address these issues in a way that young men will be able to use services appropriately.

The aims -1. to inform young men about the services they may access; 2. to discuss with them the barriers that may exist which stop them seeing the services as being relevant for them.

The outcomes -1. to increase young men's awareness of the services that exist; 2. to increase their confidence in using the services on offer; 3. to increase their ability to question some of the attitudes they have towards men asking for help.

It is at this stage only after *purpose* and desired *outcomes* have been established that we can begin to think about method and style and consider whether an all-male group is the most appropriate setting to achieve the envisaged outcomes.

2. The Public and the Private

If the nature of masculinity teaches us anything, it teaches us that young men learn very quickly that the 'public' environment is where the risks are. Whether we describe it as bravado, front or image, we see young men develop a layer of protection, the purpose of which is to fend off verbal and physical attacks on their masculinity.

The implications of this for those of us developing practice are that, if young men feel they are in a 'public' environment, they are much less likely to talk openly and honestly, and are very unlikely to show their vulnerability. Alternatively, when young men think they are in a 'private' environment, they are much more likely to talk openly and honestly and are much more prepared to be vulnerable.

Many workers will recognise this difference when they see young men with their mates and when they are alone. Workers continually report that young men on their own are approachable, will talk, and be much more rounded in attitude and behaviour, whereas the same young man may change quite dramatically if his mates enter the room. Mothers report having conversations with their sons in the kitchen, where their sons may be talking about how difficult they are finding school. When there is a knock at the door (he knows it is his mates), the boy will change in between leaving the kitchen and opening the front door. He may swagger down the hall, and, by the time he arrives at the front door, his mother does not recognise him as the same person from moments earlier: he has changed – he has moved from the private to the public.

We have to understand that many young men see this 'public image' as essential for their survival. Most will report that they "have no choice": to show vulnerability or weakness would be social suicide and set them up for ridicule. We therefore have to accept the limitations of both contact and effective work in this environment. If young men feel the need to keep up a front, they will not question, or even address, the types of issues we might (and they might) want to.

If we define 'private' as a setting where young men do not feel the need to prove they are men, or keep up a front, then one of our primary tasks has to be to create environments where the pressures to prove themselves are non-existent, or at least reduced to a level within which reflections, discussion and honesty can come to the fore.

3. Creating new environments

The most common barrier that workers highlight when talking about their work with young men is the continual banter that goes on between them. Some workers will say that it stops any 'sensible' conversation going on at all: others will say that they find themselves slipping into doing it themselves. In contrast, all of those working with young men have experienced them being open and straightforward. Reporting on conversations they have had with individual young men, workers will often mention that there was no bravado, no need for the young man to prove anything, and that it was qualitatively different to when the same young man is with his mates. Workers will also report on the journey back from an event, when a conversation will start in the back of the van and the young men talk seriously about something without slagging each other off.

To enable us to intervene effectively, we need to understand what is different about these situations and how we can recreate them, because, unless we do, groupwork (in particular) will continue to be dogged by banter and slagging.

Firstly, what is happening? Where does banter and slagging come from? Their roots appear to be in heavy industry, the trenches and the cotton and cane fields – in fact, anywhere where men have had to be able to control their emotions to survive. If we were in the First World War trenches, we may be scared, frightened and think that we were going to die, but the showing of these emotions were thought to lower morale and unnerve other soldiers and was obviously seen as a weakness. Slagging provided a release for the tension, but also helped in the process of 'hardening' men not to show how they were feeling. The same occurred in the coal mines, where the work was so physically strenuous that men had to steel themselves to keep working through pain and emotional thresholds; the work required them to be able to contain and control how they felt.

Such settings and work required men to 'learn' not to feel, for their own survival (economically, physically and emotionally). While only particular circumstances required this, the learning could not be turned on and off, and, for many men, this behaviour followed them out of their work and war settings into all other parts of their lives. The common practice of dispensing alcohol at work and cigarettes in war were also reflections of this encouragement to men to 'deaden' their feelings.

What has changed, of course, is that the work and war settings where this was required do not really exist anymore for most men, but the 'learning' still goes on. Boys are still introduced and encouraged to learn how to avoid their feelings through being able to slag off others and take being slagged. Listen to young men cussin' each others' mothers, the intention being to 'hit a nerve' and get your mate to overreact, to get angry, to feel hurt: this can develop into an art-form for some young men. Four or five years ago, slagging competitions were held to see who could trade insults best. Some people ask "How can they treat each other that way?", or say that "Cussin' is so sexist – and sometimes racist". While this is true, the (not always conscious) motivation is to harden up your mate. You don't slag off people you don't know, unless you are looking for a fight.

Even recognising the roots and the pro-survival function that banter has served historically does not make it any easier to deal with, but, if we are to work effectively, the banter has to be stopped, interrupted, avoided or minimised. The biggest problem for us as workers is that, when the banter is happening, it is unlikely that anything else can! Any suggestion of weakness would bring ridicule, and when asked why they participate in it, many young men say that they do it because they would be ridiculed if they didn't. The pro-survival function has disappeared and been replaced with a fear of exclusion.

How do we do this? How do we change the environment so that young men will feel as though they can talk openly and straightforwardly about what they think and feel? We can do this in a number of ways, for instance:

a. Offer a rule of "no slagging" – Suggest to young men that, for the duration of the session, they do not slag each other off. Our experience is that young men welcome this, and, as long as workers ensure that this rule is held to, it can create safety for young men.

b. Create special environments – When workers have thought about making environments special, young men have responded enthusiastically: youth clubs have been opened from 10pm to 1am for groups of young men who want to talk; food has been provided, encouraging young men to cook and eat, and candles have been placed on the table;

etc., etc. All such innovations suggest to young men that the setting is special, or at least different.

c. Use the van and residentials – The three environments that workers mention as those that young men "act differently" in are when they are alone, when they are in the back of a van and when they are away on a residential. While budgets can limit the number of residentials, thoughtful use of these can help to create special environments – as can work in the back of a van going to and from activities.

4. Edges of familiarity

"Where do I start?" workers ask. "How do I set up a group for young men? All they seem to want to do is activities". This is, in part, where initially thinking about method and style interferes with effective working with young men. If workers start by thinking about method and style, they are more likely to think about groupwork styles, ice breakers and other techniques, rather than about the young men themselves. Workers have been more concerned about how they can introduce appropriate groupwork technique to young men, rather than young men to groupwork.

The distinction is very important, particularly in the initial setting up of groupwork. 'Edges of familiarity' means that some thought is given to the way that young men perceive the setting that they are in. This is, at least in part, because young men will have decided very early on what the setting is for, and what they can get from it and what they can't. As workers, we have to understand how young men perceive the setting. So, for example, a young man who has decided that a youth club is for sports activities only, will approach and use it for that, not expecting to have conversation about anything other than sport, and may be surprised if other activities and conversations are introduced. If a youth club has nowhere to sit, the young men are likely to assume that you don't sit around and chat. If the office door is open and workers don't come out unless there is a problem, then young men will use this as part of their picture of what workers do and don't do.

After making an assessment of their perceptions, it is helpful to the young men if some initial sessions are used to introduce the content and method slowly, balancing between what they are familiar with and what they aren't. So, an initial session with a group of young men may be a film (nothing educational, just entertainment) so that the young men get the message that the setting can be one where you can sit, but where there are no expectations that they do anything other than be entertained. The next session may be another video, but more educationally biased, and again with little expectation of a discussion. The next session may be a game that covers some relevant issues, where a discussion is expected. Using this gradual, expansive approach leads to a building of safety and security, rather than risking the use of methods that may alienate some young men - such as ice breakers and discussions that expect young men to 'reveal' themselves very early.

This approach does, of course, take time, but this way workers are able to engage with young men, rather than risk alienating them very early on.

5. Using resources

Towards the end of this book, you will find a list of packs, posters, videos and games which have been produced to support workers developing their work with boys and young men. Most of these resources have been produced out of the recognition that workers can do with all the help they can get.

Most of the packs and games have been developed for those early sessions, when workers may be a little nervous and lacking in confidence. They have also been produced to act as a needs assessment tool. Our own *Man's World* game includes a number of questions and statements that can be used to assess levels of interest and resistance and the potential for discussion and exploration.

6. The link between feelings and movement

Vic Seidler describes men's relationship with feelings as one of antipathy. He suggests that boys are given such a strong message about not having (especially soft) feelings that, when they do feel, they feel bad about feeling.

Coupled with this, is a narrowing down of the kinds of feelings that young men are 'allowed' to show. By the age of seven, most boys have been told (and have usually internalised) that boys don't cry; that, if they hurt themselves, they would be wiser to keep quiet and not risk being ridiculed for being a baby. By nine or 10, any 'soft feelings', such as love, being thoughtful, and even being reflective, are thought of as 'inappropriate'. By the time young men are 14-16, laughter and anger are fine, but anything else is doubtful. This narrowing of feelings often means that, when young men do begin to acknowledge feelings, they will be 'funnelled' into laughter or anger. Workers will often report group discussions with young men where someone is feeling something and they (or indeed others) will crack a joke, or someone will get angry or push someone off their chair.

Within domestic violence and anger management projects, as men describe their violent acts, they find that often hurt, pain and other feelings contribute to the snap into violence – "She was showing me up, she shouldn't have made me feel that way", "I was so jealous, I snapped".

This discomfort often leads many men to want to physically move, to remove themselves from the environment they are in, to escape, but also to deal with how they feel. For many men, dealing with how they feel is not a cerebral, talking activity. Traditional counselling methods, of sitting quietly, talking and thinking about how you feel, are not ones that many men find useful. One aspect of sport and activity for men is the release of feelings. A man will return from the gym having "got the day out of my system", go for a drive when he has something to work out, or go out running when things get on top of him. Sport and activity can, of course, also be an escape from feelings and difficulties, but we can't lose sight of the reality (and potential) for some men of using these activities as a release for pent-up feelings.

Within our work with young men, this link between feeling and movement shows itself in a number of ways, through restlessness during discussions, inappropriate boisterousness from individuals, violence (and the threat of violence) towards each other and the workers, and absence when they feel under pressure.

As workers, this can be dealt with in a number of ways. We can get annoyed with young men because "they don't use the setting appropriately, and get disruptive", or we can accept that, if we expect young men to feel things, then we may need to build in some physical activity, or talk with young men as we walk with them. This doesn't mean that discussions around the pool table are suddenly the panacea of boyswork, but, when young men feel things, they may get physically uncomfortable, and then, if this cannot be managed without too much disruption, some activity that enables young men to 'catch up with themselves' and work off their feelings would be helpful.

These practice principles are intended to offer guidelines for developing practice, but also to indicate a way of thinking about masculinity. What I have tried to do (through the practice principles) is identify what the theories tell us, and what implications this has on our practice. This has been the most useful process for those of involved in Working With Men – to develop our practice through our understanding of masculinity. So, the process I am trying to encourage is that you think through the implications of masculinity and base your practice on these.

References

1. Kilmartin CT. The Masculine Self MacMillan, New York 1994.
2. Lloyd T. Young Men's Health (A youth work concern) Youth Action, Northern Ireland 1995.

Anti-sexist work with boys

Confusion exists between boyswork and anti-sexist work. Some hold the view that they are the same, others that they are two conflicting views of the same activity. It is my belief that this confusion has mitigated against the development of both boyswork and anti-sexist work.

In 1986, Kerry Yeung suggested that "the equation is swiftly being assembled: work with boys + male youth workers = anti-sexist youth work" [1]. Ten years after this article, the same equation still seems to have currency. Recently, an article in 'Young People Now' carried an introductory paragraph stating that "anti-sexist work with boys and young men often turns into an exercise in collective guilt", but what followed was a very good example of work with boys carried out by male youth workers with no mention of anti-sexist youth work [2].

Hainsworth has suggested that "a boys' work practice which does not in some way attempt to raise awareness of these issues of power, or which, on the contrary, describes men and boys in terms of powerlessness, is inadequate. As feminists have developed a girls' work practice which raises awareness of the political issues in relation to sexism and links them to the personal and internal, so boys' awareness might be raised so that they too can link their external experience to their emotional lives" [3]

This quote highlights three of the most common confusions about boyswork and anti-sexist work with boys. First, it assumes (or hopes) that the aims of boyswork are the same as a girlswork practice based on an understanding of patriarchy and a power imbalance between men and women

- which it isn't. It then goes on to suggest that we only view young men in relation to young women and sexism, which boyswork does not attempt to do. Thirdly, it suggests that boyswork does not concern itself with the interplay between external experience and internal thoughts and feelings - which forms one of the main strands of boyswork. Boyswork and anti-sexist work with boys, rather than being in opposition to each other, are, in fact, related and complementary. Their origins are the same, but their focus is different.

Boyswork has been defined as "an understanding and methods of working with young men that broadens their options and choices outside of the limitations of masculinities" [4]. Boyswork developed out of anti-sexist work with boys. Workers were having difficulty with the challenging nature of anti-sexist work with boys and the resistance to it from young men. Boyswork developed out of the recognition that at least part of this resistance was because the focus of anti-sexist work was on young women. It developed into a series of starting points and approaches which enabled workers to engage young men in general discussion, reflections on gender, and the identification of how their own lives were affected by gender conditioning.

One of boyswork's contributions has been to provide workers with understandings and approaches that engage young men and enable them to discuss, reflect and think about being men and their relationships with women. The primary focus of boyswork is on the young men themselves, and not on women; the emphasis is on the restrictions that masculinity places on their own lives, and not on the restrictions that sexism places on women's lives. These distinctions are very important, because, too often, boyswork and anti-sexist work are seen as basically the same, but having a different ideological viewpoint: boyswork is seen by some to be apolitical or part of a backlash against feminism (because it is pro-young men), while anti-sexist work is seen by some as radical or 'politically correct'.

So, that's boyswork, but what does that make anti-sexist work? Kerry Yeung suggests that anti-sexist youth work is:

"the set of youth work principles and practices which challenge sexism. Sexism being the set of attitudes, beliefs and practices which regards women as subordinate to men and gives men the collective power to undermine, restrict and control women, socially, ideologically, economically, physically and sexually. Sexism is systematic discrimination against women, both personally (as in individuals) and structurally (as a group), because they are women"[1].

Unless you share the Farrell view[5] that sexism (or as he calls it 'bi-sexism') is two-way, meaning that men are sexist towards women and women towards men (child custody and retirement ages are cited as examples of women's sexism towards men), or are an advocate of the 'men's rights' view in which men are oppressed by women[6], then you will have little difficulty with this definition. The focus remains on women, on the power imbalance and the need to change men's knowledge, beliefs, attitudes and behaviours towards women.

So why is there confusion? One of the contributing factors is the ideological divisions to be found in both academic and popular literatures which are perceived as competing over the same territory. The literature on men reflects a broad range of understandings, with one of the main distinguishing features being sexism, patriarchy and power. At one end of the spectrum are Farrell, Lyndon, the men's rights movement and others who believe that male power is not really an issue, or that it cuts both ways, or that the pendulum has swung too far and institutional power now lies with either women, or with men who are frightened or negatively influenced by women. At the other end of the spectrum are authors who understand men only through patriarchy and sexism[7].

These perspectives are reflected in the smaller field of youth work and young peoples' literature. Early writings such as Taylor[8], and more recently Hainsworth[3] articulate an exclusive anti-sexist approach to young men, while many other writers reflect a confusion about the two (in the way that 'Young People Now' has as quoted above).

With this tension, misunderstanding and view that there is only room for either boyswork or anti-sexist work with boys, it is not surprising that practice has been inhibited. How can we, then, develop anti-sexist practice with boys? How can we begin to tackle the sexism that many young men exhibit? Like most other pieces of work, we need to:

1. Understand the issue we are trying to deal with;

2. Be clear about our purpose, aims and expected outcomes;

3. Develop a strategy that enables us to deliver these;

4. Decide on appropriate methods, settings, resources and approaches that will enable us to achieve our aims.

1. Understand the issue we are trying to deal with.

Taking Yeung's definition, sexism is "a set of attitudes, beliefs and practices" - not likes and dislikes, but attitudes, beliefs and behaviours that society reinforces through its many institutions.

We therefore need to have an understanding of learning theory and strategies for changing attitudes, beliefs and behaviours. So, for example, Roediger[9] suggests that, while attitudes are 'relatively stable', they are sometimes context-specific. For instance, a young man might generally appear to be anti-sexist within a home environment where sexism is disapproved of: he might also reflect a conflict of attitudes by not behaving towards his sister (or mum) in the same way as other women; and he might then exhibit sexist attitudes when his mates are around. He may also dislike himself for reacting to other people and situations in this way. Ribeaux and Poppleton[10] take a slightly different approach, and suggest that "an attitude is a learned predisposition to think, feel and act in a particular way towards a given object or class of objects". This means that a young man can believe that women should not work (even though his mum and all his mates' mums do): the evidence does not have to affect his attitude. He may agree with everything said about equality, but he may also feel that it is not quite right. He may be anti-sexist in view, but still behave in a way that does not set him apart from other men who are sexist. Attitudes can be shallow or strong, positive or negative, but what they certainly are is complex. Couple that with what we know about adolescence and the rapidity that young people can change their attitudes, be influenced (or react to) others and have helter-skelter self-esteem[11], and this makes attitudes, beliefs and behaviour very volatile territory to work in.

While I am not suggesting that we put off the task until we know all there is to know about attitudes, etc., we do need to have some basis for our intervention and a recognition of what we are trying to deal with. Anti-sexist work is obviously complex and requires us to have at least an understanding of sexism, masculinity, learning theory and how attitudes, belief and behaviours can be changed.

Unfortunately, most of our current practice falls short of even these prerequisites. Some advocates of anti-sexist work with boys have seen 'challenging young men's attitudes and beliefs' as the main tool to change attitudes, beliefs and behaviours. They believe that, if we challenge young men's language, the way they describe women, and the attitudes that underpin their language and behaviour, then they will change. Maybe I misunderstand what 'challenge' means, but, in practice, if it is the "What do you mean by the word ****? What does that say about women?" type of challenge, then I think it is naive to think that this will bring about changes in attitudes and behaviour. Challenge is, of course, important. It helps young men understand the boundaries and the rules (such as "We don't have sexism here"). They need to know what is, and what is not, acceptable in the youth work environment, or with us personally, but let's not kid ourselves this is changing attitudes and behaviours. Let's not kid ourselves that a strategy that leads (and sometimes ends) with challenge can change young men's attitudes and behaviour and increase their knowledge.

For some male workers, 'being challenged' (usually by women), is how they themselves have learnt about sexism. Some talk about how painful this was, how difficult it was to understand what they were being told. Some talk about the guilt they felt as the pennies dropped, etc., etc. Some men have understood sexism through theory and ideology, and, for some of these, the 'challenge' worked. However, for men who do not understand the world through theory or ideology, this approach has much less value. We need to know how the men we are working with learn and grapple with other issues; this will suggest how we need to develop an anti-sexist strategy.

For some workers, this type of challenge is an important place to start developing a strategy (for others, it is more important for them to be seen to be doing something about sexism), but we have to recognise its limitations. If we reflect on two aspects of young men's lives, we will see just how limiting it can be. Young men are young: some of the fundamental cornerstones of youth work are based on an understanding of young people. We talk about the need to listen to young people; our empathy with them; our support and advocacy role for them in the mean adult world. While this is a characterisation of what we say as youth services, it is a long way from our steel toe-capped strategy for dealing with young men's sexism! We can't divorce a strategy to deal with attitudes and behaviours from this supportive backdrop we have for young people.

The other important aspect of young men's lives is that masculinity is often very raw for them. When a young man is 'fronting up' another, we often see in their eyes a fear and concern about losing face with their mates. This is real for them, and we can't pretend that, by challenging young men (particularly when their mates are there), we can expect them to respond in a thoughtful way.

2. Be clear about our purpose, aims and expected outcomes.

What are we trying to do? In terms of young men's sexism, our aims could be on a number of different levels. We may want:

- young men to stop acting in a sexist way towards young women and female staff within a youth centre environment;

- young men to be more informed about what sexism is and the way it operates in personal relationships;

- young men to reflect on their attitudes and beliefs about gender and then about sexism.

This list could go on and on, but clarity about what we are primarily trying to do will help ensure that our strategy and practice match our intended aims and outcomes.

Currently, some workers use the terms 'sexism', 'masculinity', 'gender' and 'sexuality' interchangeably. Clarity of purpose is unlikely if basic terms are seen as so similar.

Thinking through a piece of work will illustrate some of the important components of anti-sexist work with boys and the need for clarity at all stages. So, for example:

Our aims: 1. To enable young men to understand the concept of, and reflect on their knowledge, attitudes and belief about, sexism; 2. To stop young men from behaving in a sexist way towards the young women and female staff within the youth work environment.

Expected outcomes: 1. Young men to have an increased understanding of sexism and the opportunity to reflect on their knowledge, attitudes and beliefs;
2. Young men to both understand and know that sexist behaviour towards young women and female staff is unacceptable within the youth work environment.

Here we are not necessarily expecting changes in the young men's behaviour other than within the youth work environment. If we see them being sexist out in the street, the work hasn't failed, because we know that the translating of a change in knowledge (even attitude and belief) does not always lead to any change in behaviour, or, if it does, it may only result in a partial, or specific, change. The clearer we are about the details, the more realistic we can be in our achievement of these objectives, and the more we can gear the content of what we do to the targeted outcomes.

3. Develop a strategy that enables us to deliver the objectives.

Given these aims, we want to construct a process whereby an environment where young men can reflect on what they think and believe is created and their sexist behaviour within the youth work environment is stopped. Our strategy, therefore, has two components. The first is the active creation of a safe environment where young men can reflect on issues, and the second is the active containment of aspects of their behaviour.

4. Decide on appropriate methods, settings, resources and approaches that will enable us to achieve our aims.

The second stated outcome – Young men to both understand and know that sexist behaviour towards young women and female staff is unacceptable within the youth work environment requires both a containment of young men's behaviour, and an understanding of what they are being contained from doing. Our traditional means of containment have been rules: "Here, you can't do that!". While, for some workers, this flies in the face of their view of youth work, young men are not put off by rules and many are attracted to activities and environments that are very highly structured and rule-defined. For example, sport and quasi-military environments rely on rules and regulations (and an understanding and acceptance of these) by participants. Agreement on them is less important than an acceptance of them, and a clarity of consequence (if you break them) is also crucial: if you lead with your elbow in football, then you know you will be sent off. This same level of clarity about sexist behaviour and the consequences of stepping over that line are crucial within a youth work environment when working with young men.

Some workers will say, "Yeah, but they don't learn anything from these restrictions and rules", which misses the point of rules in this environment. 'Good' rules protect. Professional footballers would never play football without a referee: the 'no-elbowing rule' is there to stop some players and to protect all players. 'Good' rules in the youth environment will stop some people (quite often, young men) and protect all - they are not primarily there to enable people to learn anything. In the same way, we do not expect football players to translate 'no elbowing' on the field directly to no elbowing some guy in a pub. For many men, rules are context-specific, and part of learning about life is to learn what rules operate in which environment. Most young men do not have a major problem about rules, but they do have a problem when the sanctions are not clear, not acted upon consistently, or not acted upon at all, or when they think the rules are fundamentally 'unfair'. Again, following the football analogy, footballers don't have a problem with the rule about elbowing, but they do have a problem with the way that different referees interpret the offence. Young men's behaviour will, and does, need containing, for their (and other people's) protection. Containing their sexist behaviour will be a part of that process in all youth work environments.

Parallel with this containment, as part of the first outcome, young men to have an increased understanding of sexism and the opportunity to reflect on their knowledge, attitudes and beliefs – there needs to be the creation of environments where young men can understand what sexism is.

This may need to be broken down into a number of steps, which could include:

Step 1. A reflection on gender and masculinity - which would fall back on boyswork methods and resources, aiming to encourage young men to reflect on being men; what this means in terms of gender conditioning; and what men and women are told about being men and women. This enables young men to reflect on themselves and their own experience before reflecting on young women.

Step 2. Understanding the concept of power - the fundamental concept within sexism is of power (while the fundamental concept of gender is difference). Young men often have a lot of difficulty understanding that they have 'more power' than young women, because their own feelings are so often about feeling power<u>less</u>. Introducing the concept of power through their own experience of adultism (the oppression of the young), class or (if appropriate) race, enables young men to understand the power of institutions lives. So, for example, to ask a group of young working-class men about the way that the media, their school, the Government, views young working-class men will enable them to understand the way that stereotypes and assumptions lead to negative views, which they can at times internalise and/or fight against. The power that individuals (such as school teachers, magistrates and politicians) have in reinforcing stereotypes and discriminating against them, etc., etc., all becomes apparent to them with very little difficulty. This can then lead to:

Step 3. The introduction to sexism where the power imbalance between women and the institutions and within individual relationships, etc., can be more easily understood because of Step 2.

This 'block-building approach' on knowledge opens doors to young men being able to conceptually understand sexism and can lead to an exploration of their own attitudes and beliefs about sexism and their relationships with women.

These three steps will take time, particularly when carried out in an informal setting. Appropriate methods and resources will need to be selected, and set-backs allowed for, but let's not pretend that a 'challenge here and there' will enable a realistic anti-sexist practice to develop.

This chapter has attempted to look at the different components required to make anti-sexist work with boys a practice reality, rather than a piece of rhetoric. The work needs to be thought through, and workers need to be realistic (not setting themselves up to fail). They need to understand how attitudes and beliefs are constructed, and how they can change; how people learn; and the differences between some of the concepts (such as 'gender' and 'sexism'). All of these components are crucial if good pieces of practice are to develop.

References

1. Yeung K. 'Anti-Sexist Youth Work - What's it all about?' Working With Girls Newsletter Feb. & March 1986.

2. Burke T. 'New Man...New Masculinity?' in Young People Now January 1996.

3. Hainsworth G. 'Working with boys' in Cavanagh K. and Cree VE. Working With Men (Feminism and Social Work) Routledge, London 1996.

4. Lloyd T. Work with Boys NYB, Leicester 1985.

5. Farrell W. The Myth of Male Power Fourth Estate, London 1993.

6. Lyndon N. No More Sex War Mandarin, London 1992.

7. See, for example, Connell RW. Masculinities Polity Press, Cambridge 1995, and Pringle K. Men, Masculinities & Social Welfare UCL Press, London 1995.

8. Taylor T. 'Anti-sexist work with young males' in Youth and Policy 9, 1984.

9. Roediger HL. et al. Psychology. Little Brown, Boston 1984.

10. Ribeaux S. and Poppleton SE. Psychology and Work, an Introduction MacMillan, London 1978.

11. See Coleman JC. and Hendry L. The Nature of Adolescence Routledge, London 1990.

Raising the issues without raising the issues!

Our general awareness about gender has been raised primarily by feminism and feminist writings. Over the last 10 to 15 years, our understanding of masculinity and the changing nature of being a man has increasingly impacted on our understanding of gender and sexism.

For many of us, our own awareness has come from a direct grappling with the concepts of masculinities and gender. While this direct understanding of the issues and concepts is very useful, and certainly helps inform most of the current developing practice, this doesn't have to be the only way that working with boys and young men can stay true to addressing gender and masculinity matters.

Approaches can focus on the impact and indirect effects of masculinity, and not necessarily on masculinity itself. So, for example, we could address the skills and attributes that the experience of growing up male leaves relatively underdeveloped, but which could be very useful for young men to possess. Research, looking at the underachievement of boys in schools and their attitudes to the job market, indicates that young men too often lack skills such as:

- a flexibility of attitudes towards subject choice and gender roles;
- an adaptability to the rapidly-changing work environment;
- an ability to recognise their feelings;
- an ability to manage their feelings;
- a willingness and ability to seek help when required;
- an ability to be assertive when required.

This would appear, at least in part, to be as a result of our socialisation as boys and men, and this can be addressed and approached in a number of different ways. We could engage young men in discussions and exercises that will focus on the nature of being a man, or, alternatively, we could engage with the need to develop the skills that the experience of being a man leaves relatively underdeveloped.

This approach is suggested as a useful one, both in terms of content, as well as in terms of process (especially for young men that may not be so enthusiastic about reflecting on being a man, or within a setting where the links may be more difficult to establish, such as a work-based training environment). For some young men, the externalising of discussion and reflection towards "men in general" is helpful and very useful: for others, it is too abstract and too much like a social science lesson. Addressing the effects of masculinity on skills and attributes can be much more engaging, immediate and relevant for some young men.

However, this approach must involve workers thinking through how masculinity impacts on young men as well as what masculinity is. I will describe a short course for a group of 12 young men who had been unemployed for at least two years. This was a six-week course, and I delivered the equivalent of two days of it. I was given the brief of raising issues of gender in the workplace and of gendered work. I was told that the young men were not very keen talkers, were underachievers at school and liked the practical parts of the course most.

I opened the course by asking them about their work expectations, what they would like to do and what they thought they might get. Most of them were fairly realistic about what might be out there for them. We discussed the changes in the labour market, the growth in 'women's work'. We moved on to a series of quotes that I have from employers, who say how irresponsible they find young men;

how they find them poor employees; how they arrive late; how they complain and don't work so hard, or as well, as young women.

This was followed by a fairly lengthy discussion about whether these comments were true, whether they fitted the young men on the course, and how important these perceptions are, regardless of whether they are true or not. This is where we addressed the underdevelopment of certain skills, particularly around flexibility and adaptability (the main attributes that both schools and employers say that young men lack as personality traits).

The rest of the course focused on what these attributes were, how much of them the young men had and how they could develop them. The young men liked the development of the skills angle – they could see the immediate relevance, the usefulness in what they wanted to do. It wasn't abstract or separate from what they do and think, or the dreaded "boring".

This, of course, is just one example. Feelings management and recognition of feelings is another area where we have been developing work on the basis of skills training. Others have developed assertiveness skills courses for men, and, of course, when you move into management-type skills, they are all training courses that could appropriately be underpinned by an understanding and thinking through of the impact of masculinity, without necessarily mentioning it.

Evaluation

'Evaluation', 'assessment', 'inputs', 'outcomes' and 'purpose' are all terms that have slid into funders', managers', and even our own, language. While, for some, this has sat well within the way they have worked before, for others, they are hoping that the newspeak will pass away in the same way as it has arrived! Most of us, though, are keen to find ways of incorporating them into the way we work and have valued (even if we've also felt irritated) having to think about the impact our work has on the men we work with – about outcome evaluation.

Most of us want to know whether what we do works. Most of us want to know whether what we do is effective. Most of us believe that evaluation has an important role to play within developing services. However, that is probably where the 'most of us...' statements would have to end. Some of us are doubtful about the methods we have available to carry out evaluation. Others are unsure about 'outcomes'-led evaluation. Many discussions about evaluation become reduced to, "How can you evaluate behaviour change?", or "How can you prove it works if it hasn't been evaluated?" and "It's process we evaluate, not outcomes".

Add this to an area of development such as working with boys and young men and even bigger problems arise. Working with boys and young men has, to a large extent, grown out of a concern and considerations that have a process base. We have been concerned about the difficulties we have engaging young men away from an activity, enabling men to communicate to us and each other, enabling groups of young men to talk and express what they think and feel in an honest and straightforward way. What has often been harder to do is to go on and say why we want to do this. We fall back on the difficulties that young men have in doing these things (e.g. they can't express their emotions), but hesitate to translate this into clear, straightforward outcomes. When workers have written up their practice, monitoring and evaluation have often been confused – they have found outcomes difficult to frame and so have often relied on process; the workers' subjective experience, or how happy men were with the process of the 'group', has been proposed as an evaluation method.

Increasingly, funders (particularly for new developments) are expecting clarity of outcomes, and not process; knowledge, attitude and behaviour change, and not 'safe environments' or 'somewhere to talk'. If anything, funders are actively moving away from process measures, which they see, at best, as a means to an end, and not an end in themselves. Outcomes, effectiveness and evaluation is the language of the 90's.

When workers have defined (non process) outcomes, they have often been ambitious. This is, at least in part, understandable. Funders (and management) invite us to inflate what is realistic. When supervising workers developing work with young men, I have encouraged them to reduce their initial aims and objectives, which often make claims that they just could not achieve. One worker, developing a 10-week programme (one night a week) intended to "change offending behaviour". He thought the funders would not fund it unless it was ambitious (I think he was right), but then he was stuck with aims, objectives and outcomes that he could not achieve in the time he had.

Another problem that arises is that evaluation is seen as an add-on, or something to think about when the work is complete. Too often, workers and management ask about evaluation at the end of a project, rather than at the beginning. Sometimes, as well, evaluation is seen as part of the fund-raising strategy: "If we can show that it works, we can raise more money to support the project".

Evaluation is part of a wider process. If we do not have a clear, straightforward purpose, aims and objectives, evaluation is very difficult. If we are not clear about why we are evaluating, what we are evaluating, how we are evaluating, for whom we are evaluating, and who are the most appropriate people to carry out the evaluation, then we will have problems in effectively evaluating our work.

Evaluation models abound, especially in the USA: research evaluation, project evaluation – you name it, they have evaluated it, and produced a model to fit all circumstances. But what do we need to understand about the evaluation process, and how does it fit the work we are trying to develop? It is, without a doubt, much better to approach evaluation with scepticism. 'Round holes' and 'square pegs' are words that spring to mind - if evaluation is a science, it is an unexact one.

Having said all that, we can't ignore evaluation; we can't choose the bits of evaluation we find easier to do; we can't side-step outcomes evaluation because it's hard to think through outcomes and the instruments to evaluate them. In short, particularly in a area such as working with young men, we need appropriate methods and instruments to evaluate our work without compromising its developmental nature.

So, after the argument for doing it, what does it involve? This chapter is not intended as a guide to evaluation: however, some basic concepts and views about evaluation are essential. First a definition: how about "Evaluation is the process of determining the adequacy of a product, objective, process, procedure, program, approach, function, or functionary"? This is not to be confused with research: "Evaluation differs from research in that it focuses on judging the worth of particular phenomena, rather than obtaining generalisable knowledge or theory about a whole class or phenomena" [1].

There are two basic measures used by most evaluations:

Process (or formative) measures, e.g. "happy sheets" at training did they like the way it was taught/received, did they like the style, the methods, the way that the learning occurred?; and

Product/outcome (or summative) measures such as "By the end of the course, men will have a clearer understanding of masculinity", or "At the end of the residential, expectant fathers will be able to change a nappy, talk about their own childhood, and name at least five ways that they can help their newborn baby".

Bloom [2] has taken these two basic types and suggested that they can be used at a number of levels, so Process could start with evaluating whether participants attended; whether they responded to what was offered; valued what they were offered; and were able to conceptualise and finally characterise (where the participants take on the concepts as their own).

Then, with Product/outcomes, he suggests the different levels that could be used would be knowledge, comprehension ("using the knowledge known"), applying the knowledge, analysing it and synthesising it (putting various bits of knowledge together to form a meaningful whole).

Some models have aimed to link evaluation within a planning scheme, thus avoiding the 'latch it on the end' principle. Stufflebeam [3] suggested a "decision-making model" where context, input, process and product are all evaluated. "Context and input reflect the intentions of the program, whereas process and product reflect the actual program accomplishment". He suggests that context evaluation will help with evaluating need and ensuring that there is clarity about what is trying to be carried out and why. Input evaluation ensures that resources (people and otherwise) are used to meet the objectives.

Validity is important within the evaluation process. Internal validity is when the evaluation instruments show what they are supposed to. So, for instance, if the planned outcome relates to change of attitude, then the instrument used to measure this must measure attitude, and not happiness about the method. External validity asks whether the results apply only to the individuals being evaluated, or whether we can make a more generalised statement a fatherhood project may have worked within a Young Offenders Institution, but would the same course work with a group of dads at a Family Centre?

Some believe that the 'Evaluation Industry' has become so engrossed in its own validity and methodology that it has forgotten that evaluation was a means, and not an end in itself. Ebbutt [4] suggests a return to basics and says we should ask:

- Who is to conduct the evaluation?
- Where will the evaluator focus attention?
- What is to be evaluated?
- Why evaluate?
- When will the evaluator report?
- Who is the evaluation for?
- What style will the evaluator adopt?
- What form will the evaluation take? and finally
- How will the evaluation be carried out?

That's the theory, but what of the application and practice? This is probably best illustrated by our own attempts at Working With Men to use the tools to evaluate our work.

At the proposal time, the best judge of whether we ourselves know what we are trying to do is the ease with which we can write down the aims and outcomes of the project. Sometimes this can be done in 10 minutes, and, at other times, it can be chewed over for months. So, for example, we have developed a project within schools, raising issues about fatherhood with groups of young men. The aims of this project were:

1. to offer a responsive service to individual young men (up to 21 years), as well as access to educationally-based courses on Fatherhood (certificated), over 8 to 10 weeks. Courses will be tailored to fit the different needs of groups of fathers and those young men who are not fathers;

2. to work alongside other professional workers offering courses to young men (fathers and non-fathers) within agencies such as schools, community-based projects and social services;

3. to offer training courses to professionals wanting to develop fatherhood courses and groups;

4. to develop, test and sell resources for the development of fatherhood courses;

5. to develop a model for fatherhood courses.

The initial stage of the project's development would focus on:

a) the development of methods to assess the needs of boys and young men;

b) the offering of a series of courses, which target different groups of young men within a variety of settings;

c) the compilation, development and testing of material for use with different groups of young men.

These objectives just fell out. We knew what the project was about, and, once we had these aims, methods, style, setting, timescale and other aspects fell into place easily. There was a clarity and coherence.

The evaluation process, however, was a little more complex. Here are extracts from our first attempts to settle on an evaluation process. The descriptions are taken from our application, and the comments in italics are about the evaluation process and method:

"We are interested in evaluating three different aspects:

1. Needs Assessment

"To develop criteria to determine the points of entry and curriculum content, and will be tested and refined as this stage develops. So, for instance, we will aim to determine whether age, having pets, brothers and sisters, levels of academic achievement, voiced interest in relationship and views about the breadwinner role might determine appropriate points of entry".

We first need to have a needs assessment process before we can evaluate it! This could be a pre-course questionnaire – a reflection sheet that will concentrate on the young men's circumstances (pets, brothers and sisters, etc.) and then their level of interest, perceived expectations of the future, etc. We need to decide initially what aspects we think will influence young men's point of entry, and test those. While testing those, we will also be able to note other components that we think will impact on needs assessment.

2. Courses

It is envisaged that a number of courses will be offered, totalling up to 60 hours. These hours will range from modules within PHSE in schools, through to one-off sessions in youth clubs. The content of these courses will range from discussions about the bread-winning role, through to modules which include components such as men's and women's roles, negotiating skills, their experience of being fathered and childcare knowledge and skills. Materials will primarily aim to provoke discussion, rather than provide young men with information.

Schools and projects will be contacted through an initial leaflet mailing introducing the project, and follow-up visits to those who show an interest and others we have had previous contact with. Courses will be offered to schools, Young Offender Institutions, community-based projects and youth clubs in the London and Bristol areas (predominantly inner city in areas where our consultants live and work). The target group will be 14-18-year-old young men and the outcomes of these courses will be to:

a. increase awareness of the changing nature of the role of fathers in families;

b. increase knowledge of the role and responsibilities of being a father;

c. develop the skills and abilities of young men in aspects of parenthood;

d. increase young men's confidence in both childcare and role negotiation.

These courses will be evaluated on the basis of young men's increased knowledge and attitudes towards fatherhood".

We have some problems here, in that we will have a number of courses that are likely to be of different lengths and content. This will make comparison difficult. We will have to evaluate the individual courses as self-contained units and use these evaluations to highlight some common themes that hopefully will emerge – for instance, that the older the young men, the more or less interested they are. They can only be 'emerging themes' because we will not be able to prove anything!

We will need to evaluate through a number of instruments:

1. *A very detailed reflection form for us to complete. We may have a number of these if the course runs over a series of lessons, with one to summarise at the end;*

2. *Similar sheets for the young men which will focus both on the envisaged outcomes and their views of the materials (see below). Some of the outcomes involve knowledge and attitude changes, so we will have to build in appropriate types of questionnaires;*

3. *A process evaluation (some of which we will pick up through 1 and 2, but we could usefully get comments from the young men, in discussion form, at the end of the course).*

3. Development of Materials

"We will continue to collect materials, but also develop some (where gaps are identified), and these will then be tested and evaluated in the courses above as to their appropriateness for different groups of young men. It is envisaged that, by the end, a pack of tried and tested materials will be available for use within a wide range of settings and with a number of different groups of young men".

So, we also want to assess the materials that we use. We will have to determine (as we develop them) what they are supposed to do, so we can evaluate them on that basis. We will also need to build in a way of assessing what else the materials may do, if they don't do what we think they will!

It all sounds a bit too questionnaire and reflection sheet based, but there may not be other suitable alternatives.

Our experience of evaluation to date is that difficult choices have to be made and methods have to be thought through carefully. The example set out above raised a number of the recurrent issues we have had to address.

Do we evaluate process and/or product?

We run a fairly extensive training programme, where we have an initial, more process-based "happy sheet" to be filled in at the end of each course. This is then followed up by a more detailed evaluation completed by participants three months after their attendance at a course. Our primary concern is whether the courses impact on practice and develop workers skills: we are less concerned about whether they had a good time! We like immediate comment (which can impact on future course content), but we give much more weight to the follow-up questionnaire. These two are supplemented by a process and outcome evaluation form for the course trainer. Our concerns tend to be outcome/product-led, in part because that is usually the focus that our project funders have, and in part because they are the concerns we have.

However, in work with young men, process matters more because we have much less leeway in terms of attention span, levels of interest, compulsory attendance etc., etc. So, for courses and work with young men, we tend to take account of process more than in our training.

How much can we expect participants to fill out?

We would, on occasions, like to spend more time on evaluation than the course/training itself! The fatherhood evaluation methods were severely restricted by the time frame we usually had: if we delivered a course over a number of weeks, this could take the form of a series of hour-long single periods, and therefore evaluation of a session could only take up 2-3 minutes of the period time at most.

We think our training courses are very demanding, and so extensive form-filling at the end of a course is unrealistic, especially when we are more interested in the impact on practice. To date, we have looked at a number of evaluation mechanisms, but usually return to sheets with questions that have a mixture of numbers to circle and more open questions for comment.

Choices have to be made!

The reality of evaluation is that compromises have to be made. Primary concerns have to take precedence over desirable concerns. This has often been the biggest problem for us. We would like the young men to give us details in written form (so they can complete the feedback on their own, and in reflective mode), but the reality has been that literacy levels mediate this process, and, while a noted discussion was far from ideal, it was better than nothing.

Validity has its problems!

The fatherhood courses and materials are a good example of where we would have liked to have a validity rating. We would have liked to say that the different schools and groups of young men (we tested the courses and materials on), tell us enough to indicate that they could be replicated and used in similar environments, but we can't.

The variables are just too many, we have too little control over the young men's days, the environments we are working in and the perceptions of our work in young men's minds. So, for example, in one of the schools where we ran a fatherhood course, it went very badly. The young men played up, acted out etc., etc.: they ended up telling us halfway through the course that they were due to go on a trip (that they'd been looking forward to), but their teacher didn't think they had behaved well enough, cancelled the trip and got us in instead! The teacher hadn't mentioned this to us! This was a variable that had devastating affects on the course.

Currently, our approach to evaluation is informed by a number of basic principles:

1. Think the process through, and think it through again;

2. Decide what are the most important components to evaluate, and don't compromise these;

3. Be realistic – don't complicate or over-burden the process;

4. Be prepared to accept that it didn't do what you wanted it to! Don't blame the process;

5. Match the method with the evaluation aims, and not the other way around;

6. Think the process through, and think it through again. (– No, this isn't a misprint!).

Probably the most important aspect to get right from the beginning is clarity of purpose and of outcomes. A clear, straightforward outcome, such as "to increase the knowledge of participants in the areas of fatherhood and relationships", at least indicates measures and form. We will want to measure whether knowledge has increased, but then we will have to decide whether we want to give participants an exam, accept participants' subjective experience of whether they have increased their knowledge, or some other form.

There are no short cuts to evaluation. Thinking through the work, thinking through the purpose and outcomes, will, however, help enormously.

References

1. Mason EJ. & Bramble WJ. Understanding and Conducting Research McGraw-Hill Books, New York 1982.

2. Bloom BS., Hastings JT., & Madaus GF. Handbook on formative and summative evaluation of student learning McGraw-Hill Books, New York 1971.

3. Stufflebeam DL. et. al. Educational evaluation and decision-making in education Peacock, Itasca, Ill. 1971.

4. Ebbutt D. Signposts on the road to the bottomless pool.

Examples of practice and initiatives

While we have looked at important dimensions of developing practice, this chapter gives examples of practice. The purpose of including these is not to suggest that readers should go off and recreate them, but instead to simply stimulate and encourage through the twelve pieces of practice described here.

Developing practice with boys and young men is so varied that the examples included cannot reflect the depth or breadth of the work, but they do reflect a number of the settings, ages, and approaches that workers have developed. In some respects, this and the last chapter may not even mirror each other in important ways: these examples were not selected necessarily to reflect the perspective outlined and encouraged in the previous chapter. What you will find here are committed workers who have boldly taken the initiative and carried through pieces of work.

Each of the workers was asked to describe their practice through a questionnaire.

Mark Price
Morley Street Family Planning Young People's Drop-in Clinic, Brighton, Sussex (with additional comments from Jon Ota).

Where did the idea come from?
Through discussion with other staff from different agencies who were part of a young people's sexual health forum in Brighton. The 'drop-in' was relatively new, all the staff at that point were female reception staff, nurse, doctor.

Which agencies were involved?
East Sussex Education and Social Services Departments were involved, although the main impetus was through the Youth and Health Services.

Who provided any funding the project used?
Funding for the drop-in came from the Health Authority, the specific post to work with young men was initially funded by the Youth Service, but is currently supported by the Health Authority (through the HIV/AIDS prevention budget).

What did the project aim to do?
To develop work with young men attending the clinic, either as partners of young women or attending in their own right.

What outcomes were envisaged for the young men?

1. Access to a male worker to enable information about contraception, pregnancy, STDs and testicular cancer, to be given;

2. The opportunity to explore their understanding, responses and feelings;

3. Access to a supply of condoms.

How did you recruit the young men?

We distribute general information to all young people and offer presentations to schools, plus we have specific material aimed at young men. We have also found that word-of-mouth has been important, as have referrals from other agencies.

Men will often accompany their girlfriends when they are commencing with the pill. The switch from condoms to the pill (as the main means of contraception) is often very meaningful for the couple; he feels involved and therefore is often present.

How many were involved?

The clinic operates for two hours every week (and has done for four years). Each session usually has between 4 and 10 young men attending: of these, brief contact will be made with 4-6, and extended contact with 2.

What methods did you use?

Either 'cold contact' approaches in the waiting areas or via appointments. The mere presence of a male worker is not enough. The choice between walking into a room where a strange man is waiting to 'offer' information, advice and support, or pretending to read Cosmo while checking out the 16-year-old opposite, may well be a choice between the devil and the deep blue sea, but Cosmo always wins. So, in some ways, men need to be engaged, and the impetus needs to come from the worker. Techniques more frequently used in detached youthwork are more appropriate when trying to strike up a conversation with a young man in the waiting room – just something very simple, like giving out a 'safer sex' pack with 2 condoms and a leaflet about HIV, or emergency contraceptives, may lead to a discussion or questions being asked. Even if it doesn't, they will at least leave the clinic feeling that their presence was in some way acknowledged, and also take away something (information and condoms!) that they can share with their girlfriend.

What content or curriculum did you use?

The initial contact is usually worker-led and consists of raising awareness of general sexual health issues relevant to young men. The topic areas normally used are:

- HIV / AIDs and other STD's looking at the needs for condom use;

- emergency contraception ensuring young men know of its existence and when it might be necessary;

- testicular self-examination.

About a third of contacts will be more in-depth, requiring privacy. These are often led by questions that young men ask, normally about the contraceptives used by their girlfriends. When young men accompany their girlfriends for a pregnancy test, or for emergency contraceptives, then the contact is going to take on a more supportive nature, calling for a less directive approach. Other issues that regularly come up are condom failure, relationships and sexual pleasure. It is these types of contacts that highlight the necessity for targeting men in family planning clinics. Despite the fact that they do not identify the need to speak to anyone, the levels of anxiety around sexual health issues are enormous, and, without this pro-active approach to engaging young men, these anxieties may never be heard or addressed. There is also a limited exploration of bisexuality and homosexuality in some cases.

How well did the project do in meeting its aims and objectives?

The numbers of young men attending have never dramatically increased... nor, on reflection, would we have wanted this. The project has succeeded in consistently working with those young men who attend, and, in a limited number of cases, there has been extended contact, sometimes beyond the regular session hours.

How well did the project do in meeting the outcomes?

Outcomes in terms of 'access' and 'opportunities' have been successfully met. After the first year of the project, a general target number of contacts was set by the worker at 2 'in-depth' contacts per week and 4-6 'casual' contacts. These outcomes have, more often than not, been met. This identifying, albeit informal, of the level of operation and success in terms of outcomes has been important, especially in terms of the (at times) cultural isolation of a male youth worker working within an all-female staffed health service setting.

What did you learn?

To be realistic about the scope of the project; that youth workers have a real and valid role to play in 'health authority' settings; that clinics offer specific, but restricted, opportunities to develop informal education work; and that young men often regard health service clinics as being 'women's places' and this can too often be reinforced by the provider.

Any surprises?

The levels of trust many young men are prepared to give after initial contact.

What has this work led you to do?

To look at developing alternative strategies and methods for sexual health work with young heterosexual and gay young men.

Any other comments?

The work is still regarded as being a bit of a 'bolt-on' extra to family planning work. We have continued to look for funding from the family planning services.

What would you say to other workers about to develop a piece of work?

Think carefully about the physical logistics of the setting

where are you going to be based? How will you approach young men? Make sure you develop good relationships with the manager and reception staff.

Contact: Mark Price
Young Men's Sexual Health Project,
52 Clyde Road,
Brighton BN1 4NP,
East Sussex
Tel. No: 01273-600534.

Sylvan Baker
The Rainbow Factory, Belfast, Northern Ireland.

Where did the idea come from?

The idea arose out of the success of the Rainbow Factory's all-male dance class OFF BEAT and the discussions that developed within the class.

Which agencies were involved?

The Rainbow Factory is a School of Performing Arts, where drama workshops and opportunities to develop performance skills are available to both young men and women.

Who provided any funding the project used?

Funding came from the Young Men's Health Project, which was a joint initiative between Youth Action and the Health Promotion Agency in Northern Ireland to support short-term initiatives with young men.

How did you recruit the young men?

Young men from the existing Rainbow Factory membership, aged from 11 to 19 years, were invited on the basis of their interest and willingness to see the project through.

How many were involved?

18 in total.

What did the project aim to do?

To introduce a group of young men (aged 11 to 20) to some of the concepts and debates surrounding the issue of masculinity, which would then lead to the development of a piece of theatre that could be used as a basis for peer education with youth provision.

Its objectives were to identify a suitable group from within the Rainbow Factory and provide them with an environment where they could discuss openly their thoughts and feelings about masculinity, and to help them to create some dramatic interpretations.

What outcomes were envisaged?

For the young men - an increased awareness of themselves in relation to masculinity and being men, and a positive experience with other young men.

For the workers - an opportunity to develop youthwork skills and methods of enabling young men to explore personal issues.

What methods did you use?

While the Rainbow Project has a lot of experience of working with young people, the relationship is usually one of director and actor, or teacher and student. This project offered the opportunity to depart from this product-oriented relationship, and to concentrate on a more informal approach where young men could talk about themselves.

There was a series of informal meetings in our usual performance space, culminating in a one- night-and-day residential.

What content or curriculum did you use?

This was kept very simple. We did very little other than discuss two questions:

i) what it is to be a man in today's society, and

ii) when does a child become a man, and what defines this?

How well did the project do in meeting its aims and objectives?

The project was extremely successful, allowing all its participants equal voice in debate, irrespective of age. Within the Rainbow Factory, there is an expectation that young people will give of themselves and engage with issues related to performance material. This probably contributed towards the young men's ability to spend so much time discussing just two questions – they were prepared to look in depth. The questions also provided a basis for the opportunity to translate some of this discussion into theatre that may, in time, become part of a Peer Education project.

How well did the project do in meeting the outcomes?

The project allowed participants to explore the issues and derive support from each other while explaining their own attitudes to the issues raised.

A number of the boys said that the discussions had changed their relationships with themselves, each other and their mothers. This was one of the most interesting parts of the project - whether this was because of the young men themselves (many of them being articulate and able to reflect), the setting (within the Rainbow Factory) or the content of the discussions, it is difficult to say, but the impact seemed to be profound.

The boys wrote some notes about the residential, which included:

"It was really fantastic. We talked about topics for extremely long periods of time until we decided whether or not they should go on our list of 'what you must have to become a man'. Around 10 topics were on our final list: these included 'responsibility', 'experience', 'emotions' and 'self-awareness'. Although they were all important, we all decided that the most vital thing towards becoming a man was puberty. We also discussed a lot of things – 'courage' we discussed for half an hour, but decided not to put it on the list. I really do think that this project should become a permanent thing, because I personally think that it's about time that young men got to talk about their problems".

"We did agree on a lot of things, but not without a lot of shouting and a lot of sweat being shed... I think we argued quite a lot, and sometimes I thought that, when the session was finished, some of us had come out with a lot of mixed feelings. We also played pool and listened to a lot of Michael Jackson and, oh, we ate quite a lot!".

There was also initial scripting of a revue-style piece, but, as yet, funding and scheduling has not allowed for further development.

What did you learn?

Normally, the standard set-up in which I would work with the young people was as 'director to actor'. Basically, this means that, though there is a general level of debate on issues arising, the overall decisions about matters are made by the director. And are not always made with complete agreement of all the cast – more likely by majority.

In this project, I was able to be purely a facilitator, which, to my mind, meant that I provided a measure of security and freedom for all the participants, but was not the 'driving force' for debate. Moving into this role allowed the participants to see me in a different light and meant that almost all perceptions of established authority were removed, insofar as my input was just as valid as everybody else's, but no more so.

This allowed me to alter the level and the complexity of the relationships I had with the participants to levels that still operate now, some months after the project has finished. It means members, after working on the Young Men's Project, feel able, where appropriate, to seek advocacy on pastoral matters.

On a purely artistic level, the measure of overall security and positive reinforcement has led participants to expand their interest in movement and dance to the level that they are now performing in a citywide dance project for the festival at Queens, and are happier to attend mixed dance classes and not feel self-conscious.

Any surprises?

The level of support the participants gave each other and the work.

What has this work led you to do?

The confidence the project gave me has enabled me to impact on the whole Rainbow Factory membership in terms of boy/girl and young men/women interactions. Some of the issues have been developed in a play called 'The Thin Line' which was performed in April 1996 as part of a major youth theatre festival.

Is the work written up and/or evaluated?

Only as part of the Young Men's Heath Project publication 'Young Men's Health - A Youth Work Concern'.

What would you say to other workers about to develop a piece of work?

I would say that the fundamentals of the exercise of creating an environment of safety, and maintaining this, allowed the difficult issues to be raised and handled. The work showed me that boys and young men have a lot to say, but they have insufficient opportunities to say it: also, that they feel powerless to create those opportunities for themselves. Many of them said that they could not imagine the discussions we had going on at school.

Contact: Sylvan Baker
The Rainbow Factory,
Youth Action NI,
Hampton, Clenmachan Park,
Belfast BT4 2PJ, Northern Ireland
Tel. No: 01232-760067.

Paul Brown -
working with young black men.

Where did the idea come from?

The original idea came from Catalyst Theatre in Health Education Company.

Which agencies were involved?

Catalyst, North Birmingham Community Health Trust, schools and youth service.

Who provided any funding the project used?

All of the funding was provided by North Birmingham Community Health Trust.

What did the project aim to do?

The project aimed to take a group of young men through a process where they were the main focus and their opinions and attitudes around "being male" were explored. Secondly, we wanted to produce a resource for work with young men that was proven and transferable.

What outcomes were envisaged for the young men?

1. An understanding of the range of issues that affect their lives;

2. The ability to look at and explore issues of masculinity, sexism and homophobia;

3. The opportunity to meet and work with their peers on these issues;

4. The opportunity to develop a resource for use with other young men.

How did you recruit the young men?

The young men were recruited through schools as part of their work experience placement. All the young men had selected this project, and it was made clear to them that they would be involved in various activities that looked at issues of being young men and at masculinity.

How many were involved?
10 in total.

What methods did you use?
During the two-week block, a range of discussion, drama and improvisation was used to enable the young men to talk, discuss and reflect on their lives.

What was the content or curriculum within the project?
Over the two-week period, the young men raised a number of issues related to the theme of masculinity: young men all face issues of masculinity regardless of their race, but there are clearly added dimensions that relate to being black. These were acted out through the development of scenes that contributed to a video produced at the end of the two weeks.

Racism was the major preoccupation of the group, although originally it was not part of our agenda (as our role was to examine issues of masculinity). From Day 1, when the young men were asked about major issues that affected their lives, racism was raised. This was reflected in scenes on mixed relationships and on racism in a school setting.

The school scene gave an account of the racist attitudes of teachers as encountered by this group. The two scenarios involved an incident over school lunch, where a teacher made statements to a group of black pupils about not using knives and forks to eat burgers and chips. The implication for the pupils was that black people were ignorant and unable to use knives and forks. The other scenario was the singling out of black pupils by a teacher, which ultimately resulted in their exclusion from class. The young men asked us repeatedly, "Why are they like that?". We understood this to mean, why did professional and educated people (who their families had told them to respect) not have respect for them? It was essential that both facilitators recognised racism in their everyday life. It became apparent that the young men didn't know how to deal with the situations, or the emotions raised in them.

During a discussion about sex, they started to talk about pornography, and then masturbation. The black youths all felt masturbation was wrong, and claimed that at no time had they ever "wanked". At one point, both facilitators were asked a direct question by the young men: "Do you do it?". Both facilitators replied in the affirmative, much to the surprise of the young men. Despite this openness and the fact that the facilitators had apparently sanctioned masturbation, the young men still felt it was wrong. A general comment from the young men was, "Why waste your seed?".

Through discussion, the facilitators probed the young men's attitudes further. Did they have wet dreams? Did they get erections? What did they do about them? etc. The young men's reply was that they had "dick control" and therefore denied experiencing any unwanted sexual arousal. The facilitators then asked about pornography and whether any of the men experienced arousal looking at magazines. The collective response was no, at which point a facilitator suggested he pop next door to the petrol station, buy some pornographic magazines, and, as a group, we would read them, look at the pictures and observe whether or not anyone got aroused. The response from the young men was immediate and united sometimes, it appeared, they did experience uncontrollable erections, but they insisted at no point did they masturbate.

Homophobia was a major stumbling block with the young men, as they were all (openly and, at times, aggressively) homophobic. This started on Day 2 and resulted in the young men questioning the sexuality of the facilitators. The young men could not accept that the facilitators believed homosexuality could be a personal and positive lifestyle and, as such, should be respected. The logical extension for the young men was to question the facilitators about their sexuality, and, although their response was that they both lived with women, the young men chose not to accept this as confirmation of their heterosexuality. Over the next two days, there was a noticeable lull in proceedings as the young men questioned the purpose of the project as a whole. They were uncomfortable with the issues and needed reassuring that homophobia was not to be the major focus of the project.

On a later day, the facilitators raised the issue of the black young men (an oppressed group) as oppressors. How could they oppress gay people, when they themselves had experienced, and were angered by, racial oppression? This was accepted on one level and the general feedback became, "It's OK for gay people to exist, so long as they don't come near me".

The young men not only believed that being gay was wrong, but to be black and gay was a contradiction, and, if you were gay, you couldn't be consciously black. This was the only part of the project where we felt we gave up and didn't push. While not suggesting that black communities are more homophobic, this is an issue that needs to be raised with young black people, and how this is raised needs careful thought.

During one session, the issue of peer pressure was raised. The young men all failed to see how peer pressure affected them and how they contributed to pressurising their peers. This dialogue continued for some time, until one facilitator moved invisibly into a roleplay exercise around peer pressure and fashion. He asked the group for advice on which trainers he should buy, as he had seen a pair of HiTec trainers that he really liked and they were only £25. "Move dat!" came the collective response: "Nah man! HiTec are rubbish!". It was apparent that these young men would not be seen under any circumstances wearing the wrong brand of trainer. After some dialogue in which the facilitator pointed out that he only had limited finances, the young men offered him advice on where he could purchase acceptable trainers for under £50.

How well did the project do in meeting its aims and objectives?

Over the two weeks, the young men moved from a position of distrust and frustration to a position of commitment and enjoyment. This occurred within the context of some very difficult soul-searching sessions. Apart from the production of the video, the young men also came back after several weeks to a weekend workshop to produce a set of posters. I feel the overall aims and objectives were met.

How well did the project do in meeting the outcomes?

Well, in that there was clearly a shift in the position of the young men by the end of week two. Issues that they had never discussed before were discussed openly and frankly with the facilitators.

What did you learn?

Clarity and confirmation as to the issues that young men feel are important to them. Issues about black men and homophobia were confirmed, yet issues about young black men and use of condoms were challenged. Also how young black men clearly saw masturbation as wrong, against the Bible, a waste of seed, and an activity they would take no part in.

We also learnt about the way the young black men often had to change and adapt to different people and situations. While acting out a classroom scenario, there was a need to respond in an acceptable way to the teacher, while not losing face with their mates. The teacher says, "Take your hat off". The young man has to remove it, but does this in such a way that he shows his resistance, thereby maintaining the respect of his peers.

This piece of work gave us some insight into the pressures on young black men. Within black culture, there are clear boundaries about what is, and is not, acceptable in relation to being black and male. To be black, you have to be strong in mind, body and soul and, as such, conform to what is seen as 'right'. The opportunity is, quite often, not there to challenge the accepted norm without exclusion from the security of being black.

Many young black men depend and rely on partnership, camaraderie, and friendship; the fear of exclusion from peer groups often means that young black men will not risk upsetting the norm. Ultimately, this exclusion could mean individuals exposing themselves to dealing with issues of racism on their own. When working with young black men, workers have to be aware that questioning of issues around masculinity may be associated for the young men with deeper issues of survival.

Any surprises?

The high levels of openness. Their ability to discuss some very sensitive issues, and their high levels of commitment.

What has this work led you to do?

A video has been produced. The project has been repeated, and a radio programme was made. From the project, we also have a number of photographs that will become the basis for a set of posters.

Is the work written up and/or evaluated?

An article appeared in Working With Men (issue 1995/2) and a report of the work was produced for the funders.

Any other comments?

This was an exciting piece of youthwork with a group of young men using groupwork and Theatre in Education methods in order to enable the young men to express issues of concern to them. Although hard work, it was well worth it.

What would you say to other workers about to develop a piece of work?

Work with young men will never be easy – it takes time, planning and commitment, as well as a level of skill and understanding. Don't be afraid to make mistakes, as this is all part of the learning curve. Treat young men with respect and ensure you are clear as to why you are working with them. Set clear boundaries and never collude with them in order to be accepted. Look for areas of support which may be from female colleagues.

Contact: Paul Brown
c/o Camden Youth Office,
136 Chalton Street,
London W1 1RX
Tel: 0171-388-2011.

Carl Balshaw and Jim Rowe
working with young men who have a learning disability.

Where did the idea come from?

Three of the young men had been members of a mixed sexual health/HIV prevention project organised by Barnado's Sexual Health team from Liverpool - this work was being done with the South Ribble Family Support Barnado's Office.

Which agencies were involved?

Initially Barnado's, then the Youth and Community Service through the work with the young men's team.

Who provided any funding the project used?

The Youth and Community Service.

What did the project aim to do?

Having identified particular problems young men who have a learning disability have with relation to personal and sexual relationships, the aim was to increase awareness and develop support.

What outcomes were envisaged for the young men?

1. Greater awareness of sexual identity and a recognition that these young men could be sexual (there is still a generally held assumption / belief that people with a learning disability cannot / shouldn't be sexual);

2. Learning about appropriate behaviour;

3. An ability to decide for themselves what is acceptable with regards to touching and hugging. This includes understanding when someone else says "No", and being able to say "No" themselves;

4. Improved family support and understanding of the issues involved;

5. An enjoyable, safe environment conducive to learning and development.

How did you recruit the young men?

We had already been working with them on outdoor activities - issues to do with relationships, sex and appropriate behaviour surfaced when we were away on an overnight camping expedition.

How many were involved?

One full-time and one part-time youth and community worker, with 11 young men. Three of the young men with learning disabilities worked as a small group 80% of the time, as there was a need to develop trust and confidence. The other eight were non-disabled, who met on four occasions and when hosting a group of Dutch youth workers.

What methods did you use?

We used games, discussions, exercises, full-size body maps, personal material brought in by young men (i.e. soft porn magazines, music, scrap books) and joint sessions with a larger boys group.

What content or curriculum did you use?

Social and recreational activities and group discussions about sexuality and gender; disability; relationships; friends; family and themselves; sexism and independence.

How well did the project do in meeting its aims and objectives?

The project ran for six months and realistically only just managed to scratch the surface. At this point, the young men left school and moved to adult day projects.

How well did the project do in meeting the outcomes?

The process proved to be more useful, and, in turn, more important than measurable and defined outcomes. The process enabled talking, exploring, feelings, ideas, concepts, and was participant-led. We achieved open and honest discussion, and, at one point, an acceptance that, for some people, certain types of sexual behaviour were offensive. We also managed to explore in some depth the right to say "No".

What did you learn?

The need for this type of imput to start at a far earlier age and to be supported by parents/teachers/social workers/support staff. However, the majority of these people are frightened to explore 'adult' matters with young people they perceive to be permanently children!

Any surprises?

The level of openness, the eagerness to explore and the willingness to discuss issues, but also the need to relate everything to what they had seen on the television.

What has this work led you to do?

Discussions with adult day project staff about the need to develop this work on a wider basis.

Is the work written up and/or evaluated?

Yes, in Working With Men 1995/2.

What would you say to other workers about to develop a piece of work?

1. Start with no assumptions and an open mind;

2. Seek support and inform others who have an involvement with the young people as to the nature of the content of the work and its possible consequences - especially for school and the parents;

3. Keep your line manager informed and be sure they understand the nature of the work;

4. Don't be frightened to have a go, and prepared to be challenged;

5. Talk with others, share your experience, help dispel myths.

Contact: Jim Rowe
c/o Leyland Youth Centre,
West Paddock, Leyland,
Preston,
Lancashire
Tel: 01772-422589.

Mohamed Aslam
working with young Asian men at the Himmat Project
(Himmat is an Urdu word meaning "endurance" or
"one's own effort").

Himmat is a unique project with no known parallels in the UK. Its mission is multi-faceted. *Himmat* is a supervised centre for Asian youths of 12-25 years of age, who are mostly residents of St. John's Ward of Halifax. This ward has become poverty-ridden, marginalised and divided, marked by rising crime rates, social unrest and a perception of growing racial problems. The population is almost equally divided between white, predominantly elderly, residents and Asian, predominantly young, residents. Male Asian unemployment in the ward runs at 52.5%, the second highest in the country after Tower Hamlets in London. Social exclusion in the area is leading to the formation of a ghetto mentality and a self-perpetuating state of economic depression, poor overcrowded housing, poor standards of health, lack of social amenities, low educational achievement, neglect, decay and lack of incentive to invest.

Where did the idea come from?

The spur for the Project was a concern on the part of the Probation Service that it was failing to provide effective supervision to young Asian offenders and support to their families, and, as a consequence, some young people were slipping into serious and persistent offending. It was set up as a partnership between the West Yorkshire Probation Service and the Calderdale Asian Youth Association. The Project was established in September 1991 with a 3-year grant from the Home Office.

Which agencies were involved?

The Project was supported by Calderdale Youth Services, West Yorkshire Police, Calderdale Social Services, Youth Justice, Probation Service and Calderdale Leisure Services, all of whom have representation on the Management Committee. Since April '95, the Project was further supported by Calderdale & Kirklees Training and Enterprise Council and West Central Halifax Partnership (SRB).

What did the project aim to do?

The ethos of *Himmat* is to empower young people (mostly young Asian males), but to remain within religious and cultural boundaries. Overall, *Himmat* involves young people in decision-making, developing their knowledge, skills, attitudes and confidence. This enables them to understand and act on personal and social issues which effect their own, and others' lives. The *Himmat* staff is from the local community and fully understand the cross-cultural dynamics of the Asian youth.

The initial aim of *Himmat* was to enhance the work of the Probation Service with persistent young Asian offenders, but, since April 1995, the aims are:

The Youth Centre – to offer young (British) Asians opportunities to develop their knowledge, skills, attitudes and confidence, thus enabling and empowering them to decide their own future;

Probation Work – to ensure young (12-25) Asians are effectively steered away from persistent, or serious, offending into work, or other creative and community-building activities;

Homework Support – to facilitate the social aspiration and progress of Asian youth.

What outcomes were envisaged for the young men?

1. Reduction in their anti-social behaviour;

2. Improvement in their individual achievements;

3. Increased confidence to voice their views freely;

4. Increased ability to study, and improved school attendance and behaviour;

5. Successful completion of their Probation or Supervision Orders.

How do you recruit the young men?

Crime Prevention Work: The Project base is a youth centre in the heart of the Asian community. It is open four evenings a week. The average attendance is 40 per session.

Probation Work: The probation clients are referral by the Probation Officers/Youth Justice Officers. In the majority of cases, the clients are known to the Project through its youth centre.

Homework Support Scheme: These are pupils who are targeted from the three local secondary schools. The pupils selected are in year 10 and are projected to attain 'D' grade at GCSE.

Bridging the Gap (Employment): *Himmat* and its related youth activities provide a point of contact for the local youth. We run a supported Job Club eight hours per week. This jobsearch / job-ready facility, provided on an outreach basis, has access to young people, some (but not all) with a criminal conviction.

How many were involved?

The Project has about 10 Probation clients currently, but the contract is to work with 12 clients a year. The Youth Centre runs a boys debate club every Wednesday evening: the numbers range from 10 to 18. The *Himmat* Project also runs residential events: this year, so far, we have run three - total participation 72. These residentials provide me with an opportunity to do some boyswork with the youths, especially in the evenings.

What methods did you use?

Probation Work: One-on-one using roleplays, different scenarios, case histories.

Youth Centre: Residential groupwork, usually facilitated by two workers, debates.

What content or curriculum did you use?

Probation work: The work with Probation clients is dictated by the contents of the pre-sentence report. But, in general, these are some of the topics covered:

1) Men and Men's work (Masculinity Training)

2) Power and its effects / Racism-Discrimination / Prejudices

3) Emotion

4) Assertion training, including anger management and confidence-building

5) Relationships and better understanding your own culture

6) Offending behaviour / Men and Islam

7) Drugs / HIV AIDS

Youth Centre and Residential: The issues chosen for the boys debate club are usually based on current topics. So far this year, the debates have been on:

a) "Pakis, Niggers, Honkys"

b) When did I become a man?

c) Arranged marriages

d) What is anger? / Is anger good?

e) Men's role Gender issues

f) Why do we hurt people?

g) Is it okay to show emotions?

h) What is racism?

How well did the project do in meeting its aims and objectives?

Re-offending by clients on Probation Orders has been dramatically reduced. The Crime Prevention Initiative has kept some youths who were at risk away from the street.

The Homework Support Scheme and the Youth Centre have certainly enhanced and improved attainment, outshining the statutory services seeing young Asian men.

All output targets are about numbers of people worked with and numbers attending the Project. We have succeeded in reaching all of the targets, and, in most cases, have achieved up to 50% more than the contracted outcomes. More qualitative factors have not, as yet, been evaluated or measured.

What did you learn?

The youth the Project works with – young Asians – is like working with any other British youth, but these youngsters have a different culture and religion. The culture plays a very important part in their lives. Any work with British Asian youngsters must be culturally specific and religiously sensitive.

Any surprises?

Yes, once the denial is eliminated from these youths, then they have the same problems, concerns, fears and doubts as any other white / black youths. Some of the statutory and voluntary agencies have little, or no, awareness of the cultural dynamics of Asian communities that they work with. In some agencies, workers are not even aware of the naming systems of their client group.

What has this work led you to do?

In October '95, *Himmat* was given a six-month contract by Bradford Probation to set up a project in the Toller Mannigham area of Bradford to work with Asian offenders. The contract has been renewed for another 12 months, with another contract in view. The Project in Bradford is called "Ummid" (Hope).

Himmat is in talks with three prisons and two secure units in order to offer its services at these establishments.

What would you say to other workers about to develop a piece of work?

If any worker wants to develop a piece of work especially for Asian men, one must look at the work to be undertaken with a culturally specific perception. The piece of work developed would be both culturally suitable and used for all men because "Men are men" regardless of where they come from.

Contact: Mohamed Aslam
Himmat Project,
Lord Reglan,
36 Hanson Lane,
Halifax, HX1 5NX
Tel: 01422-348045.

Mark Price
working with victims of bullying in schools in Brighton, Sussex.

Where did the idea come from?

Reading around and talking to teachers. Ongoing discussions with personal, social and health education advisers focused the idea, also discussions with young people in youth centres and projects around Brighton and Hove.

Which agencies were involved?

Youth Service, Education Department (PHSE advisers) and the two targeted schools.

Who provided any funding the project used?

Initially, the Youth Service, and then 'Safer Cities' Home Office money.

What did the project aim to do?

To explore with young male victims of bullying (age 13-16) theirs' and others' responses to bullying, including coping strategies and peer support.

The levels of self-image and assertiveness are incredibly low for a group of 14-15-year-old boys. In most young men of their age, the macho shield has already been well-developed through a range of aggressive strategies, so that fear and vulnerability is well hidden.

What outcomes were envisaged for the young men?

1. A reduction in their sense of isolation;

2. An increased feeling of confidence;

3. A sense of effectiveness in communication with schools as to their perceptions / experiences;

4. An increased social network for the young men being worked with.

How did you recruit the young men?

The schools targeted specific young men. Initial discussions took place between project staff and heads of year, who then approached identified young men. Project staff then came into school to meet with potential young men. The school followed up with letters to parents /guardians where participation would be outside school hours (N.B. several 'drop outs' occurred at this point, either by young men themselves, not wanting letters to be sent home, or by parental permission not being given).

How many were involved?

Groups varied in size from two to eight young men.

What methods did you use?

Groupwork processes, discussions, activities (some related to the issues of bullying some completely unrelated). All sessions began with a "good news / bad news" slot - things that had happened over the last week. Usually, this was followed by some kind of focussed activity. Sometimes this was abandoned in order to deal with something that arose from the good news / bad news sessions.

In all groups, about halfway into the group's life, we had a 'tell your story' session. This was always the most moving and painful, but also where often the most movement and sense of release took place. The emphasis on all processes was "don't deal with it on your own" finding allies, either peers or adults, was encouraged.

Holding the 'safety' of the groups was crucial. At times, there became a danger of scapegoating within the group - the 'hot potato' scenario, where, in order to protect yourself, you dump or deflect on to someone else. This usually involved me making sure it was me holding the potato!

What content or curriculum did you use?

The groups were fixed in time two to six sessions, depending on schools' / my availability. All groups looked at common experiences of bullying and victimisation; compared experiences at school to those at home; (to some extent) looked at assertiveness and vulnerability; and gave feedback (usually via me) as to the effectiveness of school responses. Some groups had more of a social function.

How well did the project do in meeting its aims and objectives?

Out of the sessions came the clear message that continual bullying, intermittent threats and abuse systematically wear down the victims' self-esteem and leads to feelings of inadequacy and powerlessness. This can lead to abuse of self or others by the victim in order to alleviate these feelings. For young men, attacks on their physical and sexual identity are among the most damaging forms of abuse.

The most unsafe places identified in the school by far were toilets. Extreme steps are taken to avoid using the toilets outside lesson times. This results inevitably in high levels of stress. This situation could be improved by much closer supervision of the toilets by staff.

Trust in peers and staff was identified as a basic necessity in reducing bullying, and the acknowledgement that everyone within a school shares the responsibility for maintaining safety.

How well did the project do in meeting the outcomes?

It was very successful in terms of giving young men space and a voice to be heard. The sessions succeeded in providing space for victims to have their voices heard, a necessary step in the healing process. Specifically, all participants spoke of feeling less isolated. Friendships outside the group(s) were established and support offered to each other outside the sessions.

The impact of "feeling that you can do something" was acknowledged as being important. To this end, credit card-size guides to 'safe on the streets' were produced for distribution by group members.

What did you learn?
Not to rescue young men!

Any surprises?
The high levels of disclosure by young men.

What has this work led you to do?
I want to do more of this, and also develop work with perpetrators.

Is the work written up and / or evaluated?
Some local newspaper articles and as part of a University of Reading evaluation of other 'Safer Cities' work in Brighton.

Any other comments?
This has been some of the most touching and rewarding work I have done.

What would you say to other workers about to develop a piece of work?
Spend time carefully exploring aims/methods with significant staff in schools.

Contact: Mark Price
52 Clyde Road,
Brighton BN1 4NP,
East Sussex
Tel: 01273-600534.

Ken Harland
young men's health: a youthwork concern?

Where did the idea come from?

A view that any work with boys and young men should begin with a needs assessment that involves discussions with young men.

Which agencies were involved?

This was part of a young men's health initiative set up by Youth Action (Northern Ireland) and The Health Promotion Agency (Northern Ireland).

Who provided any funding the project used?

Northern Ireland Voluntary Trust, Youth Action and The Health Promotion Agency.

What did the project aim to do?

To find out from young men aged 14-16 years their perceived physical, social and psychological needs, which workers could then respond to.

What outcomes were envisaged for the young men?

1. Opportunities for young men to reflect on and talk about their needs;

2. Opportunities for young men to communicate their needs to professional workers;

3. To identify changes in the way that young men think and feel;

4. To begin to explore ways in which services can respond more appropriately to the needs of young men.

How did you recruit the young men?

Through my own youth centre and contacts with voluntary and statutory agencies. Young men were recruited from South and West Belfast (both Catholic and Protestant). The young men interviewed included club users, non club users, young offenders and young men with contact with community groups.

How many were involved?

25 young men in total.

What methods did you use?

30-minute taped interviews with a semi-structured interview format.

What content or curriculum did you use?

The content of the interviews was discussions about areas including school, expectations of work, being a man, how they dealt with their feelings, who gave them support, their relationships with their fathers, and was aimed at teasing out needs.

How well did the project do in meeting its aims and objectives?

The young men had plenty to say and were willing to say it! The information was gathered over a three-month period and demonstrated the benefits. The interviews revealed that young men have needs that they do not express openly, such as how they seek support, job preparation and training in areas such as parenting. The findings also provided valuable information on how current youth provision can better respond to the needs of young men.

How well did the project do in meeting the outcomes?

Many of the young men commented on how seldom they are asked about what they think and feel, and what they believe to be their needs. In this capacity, the young men were able to communicate effectively to a professional worker.

What did you learn?

I learnt the importance of having quality support and guidance (the earlier interviews were very stilted and I found it difficult to get any sort of flow in both the questioning and the responses from the young men), also not to have pre-conceptions of young men's needs. That, given the opportunity, the young men will speak, and, in fact, have plenty to say.

Any surprises?

Young men's willingness and ability to speak about their feelings generally and their fears in particular; their willingness to be vulnerable; their awareness of the changes occurring in society (for example, changes in the job market and in relationships between men and women); their lack of awareness of agencies that are there to service them (such as advice and educational services); and their ability to survive.

Is the work written up and / or evaluated?

The work has been written up and published by Working With Men, titled Young Men Talking, and is also contained within Young Men's Health – A youthwork concern?, published by Youth Action and The Health Promotion Agency.

Any other comments?

What we expect from young men may determine how effective we are at working with them. If we expect young men to be 'able to cope', 'be in control' and keep their feelings private, our intervention will reinforce this perception. However, if we expect young men to be open, caring, and able to articulate feelings, in the right environment, young men will take off their 'masks' and talk to us about the real issues in their lives.

What would you say to other workers about to develop a piece of work?

Have a knowledge of issues affecting young men; Give them opportunities to talk about their needs; Offer them support; Record and monitor the work; Seek personal support / consultancy from experienced workers; Have clear aims and objectives; Have an appreciation of issues surrounding objectives; Have an appreciation of issues surrounding masculinity, young men's health and risk-taking; Think clearly about the environments in which you want to carry out your work; Work from a clear value and ethos base; Evaluate the work and write up the findings.

Contact: Ken Harland
VSB Voluntary Services Belfast,
70-72 Lisburn Road,
Belfast BT9 6AF
Tel: 01232-329499.

Mike Farnfield
Carnforth Boys' Group, Lancashire Youth Service.

Where did the idea come from?
We have large mixed provision that has failed to meet the needs of girls and boys, leading us to develop work within gender groups, usually based on known peer groups.

Which agencies were involved?
This was a Youth and Community Service initiative carried out by Chris Wright and myself.

Who provided any funding the project used?
Funding was introduced through a change to existing use of male part-time sessions and redesignation of full-time workers' workload.

What did the project aim to do?
To get young men to look at issues affecting their lives, and to provide a forum for young men that was safe and where they were able to talk freely. We also aimed to challenge the young men's accepted models of behaviour / attitudes and to enjoy being together as a group.

What outcomes were envisaged for the young men?
1. That they would have a greater knowledge of themselves, their life experiences and their aspirations for their futures;

2. That they would have experienced a supportive and open relationship with other young men and been able to express themselves on a variety of topics;

3. That they would have a greater understanding of the way young men are perceived and how they behave;

4. That they would look back and smile in years to come – that they would enjoy the experience.

How did you recruit the young men?

Young men were recruited from the youth club as a friendship group - so the young men all knew each other.

How many were involved?

A minimum of eight, and a maximum of 13.

What methods did you use?

A broad range of methods that included discussions, roleplay, outdoor activities, board games, photography and active exercises and games.

What content or curriculum did you use?

The programme was divided into 11 parts, covering a range of issues which included heroes, power and conflict, the future, sex and gender roles, self-reflection, masculine constructs, rites of passage, fathers, friendship and sexuality. Sessions were about an hour in duration and tended to be a mixture of activity and discussion, reflection and thinking. Some of the exercises aimed to get young men to talk and reflect, such as the heroes exercise, where we produced a pile of cards which have the name of a famous man on each. Each member selected three cards and wrote on the back their reasons for choosing each card. Examples from the young men were "Gary Lineker, he was a fair footballer and never got booked", "Frank Bruno, good fighter and good fun" and "Michael Jackson, great way to earn money". The gentle build-up towards talking about themselves seemed to work well, and they were fairly open about their self-disclosures and sharing - albeit covering this up with humour.

Other sessions focused on attitudes and beliefs, such as the power and conflict session. We used the roleplay where a lifeboat is sinking and decisions have to be made about who is thrown out of the boat. The sessions revealed that the young men were able to discuss without argument; to think through the issues involved; and to come to some solutions.

Through doing this, attitudes and beliefs about power and conflict were aired.

How well did the project do in meeting its aims and objectives?

By and large, I think we had a measure of success, although some sessions went very well and others not so well, and we probably did not evaluate the sessions well enough.

How well did the project do in meeting the outcomes?

I think we had fun and we made young men think; they turned up and took part, and they were thoughtful about their work.

What did you learn?

That this work was not as mysterious as we thought; that we enjoyed ourselves and did not have to give ourselves a hard time when things did not go so well; that, the more we used our own experiences as boys and men, the more effective were the sessions.

What has this work led you to do?

We have run more groups in different settings (such as school) and concentrated much more on young men's work. We have also established a 'Men's Forum' in our District to push work forward.

Is the work written up and / or evaluated?

We have written up the exercises and our experience of the group in a report titled "A spanner in the works" and are currently producing a further report entitled "Bolt on".

What would you say to other workers about to develop a piece of work?

Have a go – sometimes we seem so frightened to fail, it can paralyse us, so go for it and have your support networks in place.

Contact: Mike Farnfield
c/o Lancaster and Morcambe District Youth and
Community Service,
White Cross Education Centre,
PO Box 604,
Quarry Road,
Lancaster LA1 3SF
Tel: 01524-35099.

Paul Allen

MaleOut (working with gay, bi-sexual and transgender young men).

Where did the idea come from?

The Lesbian and Gay Teenage Group was set up at the end of the Seventies, which was the first recognised provision in London. Work done and assessments of need made by the Inner London Education Authority (ILEA) in the Eighties informed the development of lesbian and gay youthwork. After the abolition of ILEA, Camden and Islington Youth Services took on the development of the fledgling project of North London Line. Now almost 10 years later, this full-time project has contact with about 200 young people a year. The project aimed to meet the needs of lesbian and gay identified young people under 25 years of age. Monitoring and research indicated that 95% of young lesbians and gay men would not go to a mainstream or local youth club, as it was not 'safe' enough. Until this situation changes, this hidden minority cannot be served without exclusive provision; there are now about 12 lesbian and gay youth groups in London.

MaleOut is the current group for gay, bi-sexual and transgender identified young men under 25 years of age. I have worked with it for nearly three years the male-only group has changed over the years by name and direction, pioneering the work with little or no reference to models of practice anywhere else in the country.

Who provided any funding the project used?

The project is funded by Camden Education Department, with some other funding coming from health promotion services, members' fund-raising and the sale of resources. We have about eight to 20 young people at each meeting – the optimum number is 12 – with three staff.

What did the project aim to do?

The aim of this group is to provide a safe, inclusive, empowering environment for young men who identify as gay, bi-sexual or transgender.

Its objectives are:

* To provide an inclusive group to encourage membership and participation for a wide range of young men with very varied cultural, religious, and class backgrounds, abilities and learning needs, as well as at different stages of coming out or staying out.

* To offer structured and unstructured sessions which are educational, challenging and fun.

* To provide an environment which is accessible as possible.

* To publicise the group, particularly to males from black and ethnic minority backgrounds.

* To recruit and maintain a staff team that offers a wide cultural perspective to the issues of sexuality and masculinity.

* To work to maintain a group that is open to new young people at every session.

* To involve members in the development of the curriculum and activities of the group.

* To challenge issues of sexism, misogyny and anti-lesbian attitudes.

* To increase the members' knowledge of health issues, particularly sexual health.

* To encourage members to take responsibility for the operation of the group process.

* To discourage heterophobia.

* To enable members to realise their level of internalised homophobia.

* To offer one-to-one support to enable members to participate in the group process.

What outcomes were envisaged for the young men?

The outcomes we would expect to achieve are:

1. For members to gain, or recover, a more positive identity / identities.
2. For members to experience a safe, supportive space.
3. For members to be more aware of issues related to young people from other cultures and backgrounds, gender and sexualities.
4. For members to recognise, and assert, their needs more in relation to others.
5. For members to have more confidence in themselves.
6. For members to enjoy the process.

How did you recruit the young men?

Young people come from an approximate 10-mile radius of the group. Young people travel, usually away from their `home` area, so that they would not be seen by people they know who assume they are heterosexual. Young people who are beginning to `come out` to themselves and are hungry for role models, validation and a sense of belonging seek a place to be themselves.

The London 'what's on' weekly Time Out, has ironically enabled 90% of the young men to find out about the group and make the first contact call. The publication has a gay and lesbian section, but it is not a gay publication and is available anywhere. We receive no referrals via schools or other youth groups. Over the past two years of monitoring, 95% self-referred and the remainder came with friends who are already members. The isolation of the young people is very evident if you use this figure as a guide. Over the same period, only

8% have ever been to a local, neighbourhood youth club.

The first telephone call is very important, to build trust and a rapport so that the prospective member feels safe enough to come to the group meetings. Members are encouraged to answer the telephone calls during the sessions to achieve this: members also arrange to meet new people at the local train station and escort them to the venue, walk through the door with them, introduce them to others and offer them a drink. We do not advertise the address of the group for safety reasons.

What content or curriculum did you use?

The group operates on a three-month cycle, planning a programme with members giving feedback of the last programme and offering ideas for the next cycle. The turnover of members is high (some 80% over each cycle), therefore it is difficult to retain a core group: some members come once, one or two others for years, most participate for about two months. People leaving may return, years later, when in crisis, or when they need to have additional support.

This is the current programme;-

September 26th: What we want from the group.

October 3rd: What do we want to change in our lives?

10th: Smoking – why we do / don't do it.

11th to 13th: MaleOut residential weekend to Cardfields in Essex. Themes are cultural identity, health and fun.

17th: Video and pizza night.

24th: Bitches have four legs!

31st: Friends and lovers – "what do I need from others?"

November 7th: Cultural evening event.

4th: Coming / staying out (sharing discussion).

21st: Games night.

28th: World Aids Day event.

December 5th: Visit another group.

12th: Feedback, activity ideas, planning.

19th: End of year social evening.

The curriculum priorities are determined by service level, and we adjust the programme and activities accordingly each year. We flexibly respond to issues during informal time prior to the formal planned sessions illustrated above, and use our rapport with the group members to pursue a debate or discussion at any opportunity around the curriculum areas.

How well did the project do in meeting its aim and objectives?

We monitor our work at the end of each cycle by asking for verbal feedback and offering a questionnaire for young people to fill in. This asks about learning; experiences; how safe they have felt in the group; what was the most, and least, beneficial session to them; workers then use this as a basis for a review of their practice. The feedback evidence suggests we do consistently meet our aims; however, issues of racism and cultural discrimination, which take place on a sub-conscious level, are difficult to make explicit and address. Multi-oppression is a big issue for the group members; gay sexuality is still viewed as a white issue in wider society. The issue of the mental health needs of some young people is something we have not been able to support in the group very successfully due to lack of awareness and skills to operate a therapeutic group.

How well did the project do in meeting the outcomes?

Outcomes are difficult to measure. I think we do fairly well. The questionnaire provides some evidence every three months, and other evidence comes from observation of group process, conflict and participation levels: members going out with other people after the group and making major life changes while being at the group – like moving away from parents, ending a negative relationship they have been in, starting a new relationship on different terms – and sharing this with the rest of the group. Arguing with the staff is a good indicator of assertive activity and pushing the boundaries. Black and minority group young men participate equally, in terms of attendance and group 'space', and black members express, when asked by staff, that they feel they are being heard, not marginalised. Members support, and challenge each others' values and assumptions in the group. All these are subjective performance indicators for me.

What did you learn?

We have learned to expect the unexpected, through the door or on the telephone – Essex biker men, Mensa members, transsexuals wearing flats, Asian men at the point of despair, sexual compulsives and absolute abstainers, shoe salesmen to people living in cardboard boxes, Jewish gay twins, Americans on holiday, young men battered by their fathers and just thrown out of home, people dislocated from similar backgrounds as you and me. There are no stereotypes that apply to us – forget the myths as well.

Any surprises?

How supportive gay and bi-sexual men can be to each other in a `safe` space away from a commercial gay scene which distorts the truth about gay male sexuality – the stereotypes it portrays of white, slim, fit well-dressed gay youth culture excludes many.

We are constantly surprised at the diversity of people in the group. Having myself worked for 12 years in local youth clubs with explicitly heterosexual young people, I am constantly amazed how the common issue of non-heterosexual sexuality is so bonding to such a diverse set of young people.

What has this work led you to do?

This work will continue until equality is achieved for all. However, in the short term, we are exploring working in closed groups around issues of male rape and sexual abuse. The observation that black young men feel, to some extent, the need to disown their black identity in this group may lead to exclusive groups for black gay and bi-sexual men and for men who have sex with men. The age at which young people are `coming out` to others is getting younger, therefore it may be appropriate to offer a younger age range group down to 12 / 13 years old.

What would you say to other workers about to develop a piece of work?

Be brave, take risks, be prepared to be called a 'queer' or 'batty man' in a local club. To other gay men interested in setting up a project, find support, don`t over-relate to the young people, keep your boundaries clear, and enjoy the work.

Contact: Paul Allen
c / o Camden Youth Office,
136 Chalton Street,
London NW1 1R
Tel: 0171-388-2011.

Tommy Dallas
working with young men within an activity setting.

Where did the idea come from?

Initially through reading, I began to relate some of the ideas to previous pieces of work I had carried out. I had also realised that, where I had been successful, was when competition had been eliminated from the programme and where I had introduced new challenges for young men.

Which agencies were involved?

North Eastern Education and Library Board (NEELB), the Probation Service, Youth Action (Northern Ireland) and the Health Promotion Agency (Northern Ireland).

Who provided any funding the project used?

All the agencies involved provided financial support and / or resources for the project. An initial seeding grant was received from Youth Action, NEELB provided further funding, and Probation paid an agreed sum for each of their referred clients.

What did the project aim to do?

To explore the health and personal development needs of a group of young men within an informal and supportive environment;

To establish a small group of young men (6-10) and provide a competition–free programme where health needs could be explored;

To increase the confidence of at least one part-time worker in an area of working with young men.

What outcomes were envisaged for the young men?

1. To have an opportunity to explore taboo issues and feelings;

2. To assist young men in dealing with health-related issues and problems.

What outcomes were envisaged for the workers?

1. For myself and the part-time worker, to gain experience and confidence in working with young men in a competition-free environment;

2. To evaluate some of the resources available for working with young men in particular, but in health education in general.

How did you recruit the young men?

Information was sent to local youth groups and the Probation Service, and referrals were made by these agencies.

How many were involved?

After initial discussions with a larger number of participants, we ended up with six young men and two young male part-time workers.

What methods did you use?

Small groupwork formed the main basis of the project. A variety of boyswork resources were used and participants were contracted in relation to outcomes, rather than behaviour. Participants were also involved throughout in decision-making and in taking responsibility for tasks and activities; so, for example, they were involved in deciding residential menus and planned the programme for shopping and cleaning.

What content or curriculum did you use?

The first session revolved around identifying issues by asking the group to look at a series of posters and newspaper cuttings and asking them to highlight anything which struck them. We then discussed this and the issues arising and decided on some common themes, such as fatherhood, health, sexuality and contraception.

Residential One was deliberately informal and with little structure and took place on a cruiser on the River Shannon in the South of Ireland. This type of residential was chosen deliberately to assist with slowing the pace and in taking us away from all distractions. The appropriate environment was created which lasted throughout the project.

Residential Two was in a residential centre in a small country village in the Sperrin Mountains. This was a little more structured, but still informal.

How well did the project do in meeting its aims and objectives?

The project was very effective in meeting its aims and objectives. The main criticism would be that the group was ready for a lot more by the end of the project. Unfortunately, the group proved to be less cohesive than would have been wished, due to the diversity of backgrounds etc. I was pleased that the core group of five stayed involved throughout. The young men came from different towns some 12 miles apart; some were working, some unemployed, some on probation and some part-time youth workers.

The project did, however, offer a valuable insight into working with young men; it increased the confidence of myself and the part-time staff, as well as affording all the group opportunities to explore issues which were normally not on their agenda. These included fatherhood, sexuality, emotions, feelings, contraception and morals.

How well did the project do in meeting the outcomes?

Taboo issues were explored at some length throughout the project. Feelings, when explored, proved to be the most difficult area, but were nevertheless an integral part of the group's discussions. The young men did explore a wide variety of health-related issues which gave many opportunities to dispel myths and discuss areas which were normally not acceptable to discuss within individuals' normal peer groups.

From the workers' point of view, my confidence increased, as did that of the part-timers – in being less structured and having to trust in my own ability and allowing situations to develop at the pace of the group, as opposed to having a structured residential programme.

What did you learn?

The main learning for me was feeling more confident about my abilities and skills; to be less structured in my approach to residential work; and how to allow the group to develop at their own pace, rather than at the pace of my programme or agenda. Also, the importance of moving the 'edges of familiarity' for young men was understood, as was the necessity to control my own tendencies to banter or slag when confronted with that type of behaviour.

Any surprises?

The main surprise was how easily the young men responded to an absence of sport or competition.

What has this work led you to do?

It has led me to be less structured in my work generally. I have had more confidence in supporting other workers in their work with young men, and, at present, I am investigating the setting up of a young fathers' project.

What would you say to other workers about to develop a piece of work?

Don't let fear of failure put you off. The work is not easy, but the rewards, enjoyment and learning are really worthwhile. As well as that, as we say in Northern Ireland, "the crack is great".

Contact: Tommy Dallas
        Antrim Youth Office,
        NEELB, 2a Castle Street,
        Antrim, BT41 4JE
        Tel: 01849-428003.

Chris Reed
work on the initial residential element of training for apprentice scaffolders at Outward Bound Wales

Where did the idea come from?

Initially out of a personal interest in challenging received concepts of masculinity whilst doing diversionary youthwork with young offenders paddling the rivers of Georgia and Florida in the USA, then, upon return to the UK, working for Outward Bound Wales, which had a predominantly male customer base.

In 1993, 71% of our students were male and 29% were female: we had 90 all-male groups and 7 all-female groups, and 25% of all the groups we worked with were all-male. In 1995, we worked with 2,083 male students and 770 female students. Put simply, most of our clients are male; we work with three times more male students than female students. What's more, a quarter of the groups we work with are all-male groups of teenagers, and most of these are apprentices from Ford or are apprentice scaffolders.

These groups have a reputation for being difficult to work with, yet the business is worth £100,000 per annum to Outward Bound Wales. I started to look at ways of working with large groups of (often resistive) young men that meet business and industrial training needs and still provide an opportunity for personal development for the young men, focusing particularly on peer support and self-awareness. The apprentice work, particularly the work with the scaffolding apprentices, seemed an ideal vehicle for 'boyswork'.

Which agencies were involved?

Outward Bound Wales and Erith Training developed a new 12-day programme. The Construction Industry Training Board (CITB) and Outward Bound Trust approved and marketed the new programme to training providers which do not currently use Outward Bound Wales. The two-week

Outward Bound course is the initial compulsory part of the apprentice training, and not all providers were complying with this.

Who provided funding?

CITB is likely to spend over £50,000 a year at Outward Bound Wales. Outward Bound Wales provide the time for me to develop and manage the programme for CITB.

How do you recruit the young men?

CITB recruit through schools, the careers service and national employment services.

How many were involved?

There are 30 x 10-person courses per annum at Outward Bound Wales, so about 300 young men per year (we have had one female apprentice in 10 years). With two staff per course, that can mean about 50-60 staff are involved.

What does the project aim to do?

The specific Vocational Course Aim agreed with CITB for the 12-day programme for apprentice scaffolders is 'To provide training beyond the vocational skills that will enhance employability after basic training.'

The specific Vocational Course Objectives are to:

1. Test, and improve, site fitness and physical & mental endurance;
2. Demonstrate competence in working at height and under pressure;
3. Indicate trainees' reliability;
4. Improve ability to learn new skills;
5. Provide experience and training in working as a team and dealing with other people;
6. Improve problem-solving and task management abilities;
7. Increase apprentices' ability to develop more effective ways of operating;

8. Provide a record of individual performance in these areas.

The course then provides the opportunity for apprentices to learn and apply new skills, work with others, manage projects and monitor their own learning.

The General Development Aim is:

In settings which are safe emotionally and physically, to give the young men an opportunity to experience dealing with new and challenging situations, and learn to rely on other people and themselves. Working in the construction industry is dangerous, and the idea is to help the guys start to develop coping strategies before they get on site.

What outcomes are envisaged?
For Outward Bound Wales:

To improve and maintain our market share of apprentice training by providing quality client- focused training;

To reduce and prevent the negative impact of large groups of young men on the Centre, other customers and the local community;

To develop working practices to meet the needs of other similar client groups.

For participants:

To help the young men become more effective, and to rely on themselves and their peers for support;

To enjoy and value the experience.

For the CITB:

Some idea of how apprentices manage challenging situations and pressure, and helping them find ways of managing this themselves.

What methods do you use?
We provide solid and realistic pre-course information so the

young men's expectations are realistic. We use a three-stage learning cycle. Initially, the participants are taught basic physical and emotional safety rules. Secondly, they are encouraged to modify what they have learned to become a self-managed team or teams. Finally, they get an opportunity to test this out and self-assess individually and in groups.

Outdoor activities: The programme has two major expeditions in the hills of Wales, two days of rock climbing and two days of water activities. Finally, they do the 'Big Test'. The format of this is variable, depending on the group and the weather, but comprises a series of activities to act as vehicles for them to make judgments on their own performance.

The course closes with exercises in which they are helped to make transfers from the learning on the course to the workplace, including a report which is partly compiled by staff, partly by the individual apprentice and partly by the group. This is based on a National Record of Achievement.

We work to get the groups to self-manage, for example to tell each other and agree together what is acceptable behaviour. In simplistic terms, if a young man faced with a difficult situation gets belligerent, his behaviour impinges on the other guys; if we can create a situation in which the staff and the rest of the group support him, but point out that, if he were to do this on site, he would be laughed at, the individual may then choose not to do that on site and avoid the humiliation of learning in the very public and brutal arena of the building site. If the feedback can come from his peers, the effect is more empowering and starts to encourage self-awareness and group self-management, etc.

What content or curriculum do you use?

Staff are trained to focus their groupwork and personal development practices in a way that works well with the male client group. We use a model which views the course as having four styles of working with the participants. These are the 'Formal and Informal Approaches in the Public and Private Arenas', a model developed by Chris Reed from training given by Working With Men which provides a structure for development particularly suited to working with large groups of young men. Staff are helped to consciously choose a style of groupwork or development work that is situation sensitive, rather than working the same way all the time. Young men will always have a private arena in which to express themselves and thus discourage the development of pecking orders and bullying.

This is underpinned by a Positive Discipline Programme, developed from a school setting, which simply informs the young men what behaviour we expect and what they get in return.

It works by opening doors to those that want to learn, rather than closing doors on those that don't. It is enabling rather than punitive.

For self and peer assessment, we use a set of traffic lights as a metaphoric model for what behaviour will enhance movement towards goals (green lights); what behaviour will impede progress (red lights); and what behaviour could bring about a red light if the circumstances change, or if the behaviour continues unchecked (yellow lights). The model is used where and when appropriate, and forms the basis for agreement over ground rules. Apprentices get four formal performance interviews throughout the course which form the basis for a written report at the end of the course.

How well does the project do in meeting its aims and objectives?

The training given to staff outlined above is essential; without it, the courses don't really meet the needs of the young men in a conscious way. The courses come and go well enough, but they lack the focus necessary for working with young men.

The industry has been very pleased with the balance between their need for a course to 'toughen 'em up' to the brutality of being a labourer in the cut-and-thrust atmosphere of the construction industry, and the development and groupwork needed to provide opportunity for development in a safe environment. The report is seen by many trainers and employers in the industry as a valuable adjunct to the skills training and certification, because, combined with the 'Ticket' (the certification of skills to allow individuals to work on site), it informs them of not only what the individual knows about constructing scaffolding, but what their attitude is to safety awareness and reliability; learning new skills; working with other people; project management as a team; problem-solving and self-reliance.

How well does the project meet its outcomes?
We are retaining and improving our market share. We have had few 'laddishness' problems impacting on the Centre at Outward Bound Wales, but it is still early days. We still have to formalise this and apply it to similar client groups. Young men consistently do this programme and leave having said they learned something useful, or saying it has reinforced their opinions of how to behave in the industry. Many young men remain resistive to the end, but this is now better contained and doesn't turn into sullen disruption like it can do. Doors are opened and opportunities for learning are taken by those that can take them without having that opportunity denied by the 'resistance movement'. Those that have a potential for disruption are held in a non-punitive regime which, at a very personal level, is a valuable experience for them.

What did you learn?
That actions can speak louder than words. Making this happen was part luck and part judgment, but the success of the trainees says more than sales pitches to the industry and to people sceptical of focusing on 'boys issues'. I have had to learn to be very thorough and to work round problems, rather than trying to go through them.

Any surprises?

People really want approaches like this and means of working with boys in a conscious way are needed. Initial scepticism evaporates when they see approaches that can help them in their own work. The way young men value the creation of safe arenas in which to express themselves – they latch on to the idea of taking responsibility for, and benefiting from their own self-management, and love the opportunity to talk about themselves and their lives and share learning from outside and within the course.

What has the work led me to?

More contact with like-minded people. It has reinforced my enjoyment of working with young men, a desire to develop this further and to establish a network of workers with similar interests.

Is the work written up or evaluated?

Evaluation is ongoing but informal.

What would you say to other workers about to develop a piece of work?

Be thorough and systematic in your approach, and let the work speak for itself. Don't be put off by resistance amongst other workers, or from the young men: creating a safe environment for guys to express themselves will become self-procreating, the young men will find it valuable and take it up eventually, even if the finished product is not quite what you expected.

Contact: Chris Reed
Outward Bound Wales,
Aberdyfi,
Gwynedd, LL35 0RA
Tel: 01654 767464.

Khalid Abdul Karim Mair
'Streetlife v The System': A Young Men's Conference.

Where did the idea come from?

The idea for the conference was stimulated by two factors. Firstly, The Break-Free Project was asked to review its programme offered to 17-25-year-old offenders. Within the programme is a masculinity and offending component, and we aimed to organise one or two larger events which would focus on this issue: 90% of our client group are male and 60% black, therefore we wanted to focus attention on the wider issues related to them. The second major factor was our attendance at the Youth Workers Union Black Workers Conference in Birmingham (January 1996), where it was evident that professionals were increasingly concerned about the plight of urban areas and the disintegration of the youth and community development infrastructure as a result of cuts made by local authorities.

Which agencies were involved?

The Break-Free Project, Haringey Youth Justice and Youth Service, Haringay YAP, The Asian Action Group, Wood Green Project and the Turkish Youth Association.

Who provided any funding the project used?

All groups on the organising committee were asked to make a contribution towards the costs of the conference. A presentation was made to the Haringey Youth Crime Safety Group. who agreed to support and contribute financially. North London Training and Enterprise Council were also approached initially to have a representative on the question time panel, which led to an informed discussion about their remit and the possibilities of them accessing and supporting the identified client group in terms of training, and they also agreed to support the conference financially. Both Haringey Youth Service and the Metropolitan Police also agreed to make a contribution.

What did the project aim to do?
The conference was developed as a multi-agency initiative, the thinking behind which was that, by including all agencies involved in working with young people in the borough, it would increase the numbers attending. We aimed to provide an initiative focusing on young peoples' needs, to provide young people with a forum to put across their views and share experiences, and to access information about resources locally and nationally via a resource pack. For maximum impact, it was decided to hold the conference on the same day as Break-Free's annual Employment, Training and Education Day, and to advertise both events together.

What outcomes were envisaged for the young men?
1. To bring young people together in a learning environment, to explore issues that face them in today's society;

2. To provide an opportunity for young people to share experiences;

3. To raise awareness of resources available both locally and nationally to young people;

4. To enable young people to develop strategies to successfully negotiate resources;

5. To record stated needs of young people in the locality.

How did you recruit young men?
From the end of March until the conference date in July, there were 12 meetings which included two young people's consultative meetings chaired by Break-Free Project. Both the Asian Action Group & Wood Green Youth Project young people's meetings were well attended, the former being more representative of the different agencies than the latter. A third meeting scheduled for the Turkish Youth Association did not take place. The intention was to take the idea to the

constituent groups, which would not only involve the various groups, but serve to promote the idea in the borough via young people's networks. All the organising groups gave their commitment to actively support the work and endeavour to bring groups of young people to the event.

In publicising the event, we had flyers distributed via the youth agencies, Probation Service and other professionals. There was an advert on the local radio station, as well as an interview on Choice FM arranged by the Rainer Foundation PR. Part of the strategy was to include high- profile speakers who had a vested interested in addressing the client group on the question time panel.

How many were involved?
Over 120 people.

What content or curriculum did you use?
Discussions on masculinity; different perspectives on history; presentations on developing knowledge and being responsible for your own learning; putting society (survival) into context; a debating forum where people in senior positions were asked questions.

How well did the project do in meeting its aims and objectives?
Attendance: both the conference and the Employer Education and Training Fair attracted more than 120 people (72% were male, 67% were black and 52% under 25 years-of-age). There was an expectation of at least 50 Probation clients (under 25) and groups from the various youth agencies. When the first speaker started his presentation, there were approximately 40 delegates in attendance. By the beginning of the Question Time, there were in excess of 120 in the conference area. The efforts in putting together planning meetings and liaising with agencies producing leaflets served to maximise attendance on the day.

Learning environment/opportunity to share experiences:
Originally 4 workshops were planned. As delegates were still arriving throughout the first part of the day, a decision was made to amalgamate the workshops into two and facilitate discussion. The workshops were co-run by workers from the Break-Free Project, Haringey Youth Awareness Programme, Haringey Race Unit and Paul Obinna Eme, director of Kemetic Education Ltd. (who had already given a presentation earlier in the day). In both workshops, there were discussions that could be described as potent, eliciting deep emotions around issues of race, responsibility, justice, equality, and personal development. Both workshops overran the scheduled time, which suggested that the opportunities for young people to discuss issues that relate to them in such a setting can be a valuable commodity. Feedback (both written and verbal) from those involved said they found the workshops useful and wished they had more opportunities to discuss issues.

Raise awareness - Resource Pack: The day was designed to raise awareness, not only in terms of resources, but in terms of knowledge. From the resources perspective, a pack was provided, giving names and addresses of organisations in the form of a directory along with other useful information about people's rights (such as stop-and-search and arrests). The ETE Fair agencies who attended provided first-hand information and access to their resources.

Recording of needs and views: The exit questionnaire provided opportunities for conference delegates to put their views across about the day or issues within their community in terms of being policed, council services, and education and employment opportunities.

Question Time Debate: The question time debate proved to be the forum where many attendees took the opportunity to air their feelings towards the panel. The importance of the question time debate was highlighted in the feedback given on the exit questionnaire. 40% of under 16's , 68% of 16 - 24-year-olds and 76% of over 25's said they would like more say in how services are provided. In comparision no under 16's, 20% of 16 -24-years-olds and 40% of over 25's thought they knew how to make their voice heard.

Initial questions to Chief Inspector Chris Boelrjck showed the strength of feeling about deaths in custody of young black men and concerns about how young people are dealt with by the police. This created a tense atmosphere, in which it seemed the police were to be the scapegoat of young people's frustration. An appeal to the conference floor, and an intervention by Eddie Nestor, shifted the focus on to how young people could meet their own needs. Questions to the panel were more balanced and related more to requests of finding out what was available, how to access services, and whether or not the panel was really committed to the needs of young people.

Developing strategies to enable young people to negotiate resources successfully: It was hard to measure how the conference was able to meet this aim. The Question Time session evoked strong feelings, while one of the early presentations, in which young people were asked to consider how important history was to understanding their place in society today, demonstrated that learning took place. Additionally, there was the resource pack which, in its introduction, gave some useful guidelines on how to approach agencies to successfully negotiate services. On the exit questionnaire, 99% of respondents found the conference useful and 84% said they found the resource pack useful.

How well did the project do in meeting its outcomes?
Measuring outcomes against the objectives, the conference was worthwhile, raising issues and possibilities for follow-up work. More importantly, it's what we do with these issues and how we follow up that should be our concern.

What has this work led you to do?

In looking at follow-up work, a number of individuals representing organisations (Youth Crime Strategy Group, NLTEC and the Metropolitan Police) made commitments to using their resources towards developing strategies and to support further initiatives to meet the needs of young people in the borough. In terms of taking a realistic view of future possibilities, it is important to assess what needs to be done, and also what can be done with existing resources. Hence the reason for critically evaluating the conference and the process.

What having a conference entitled 'Streetlife v The System' has achieved is bringing some of these issues to the forefront of people's minds. The process of organising the event has provided the agencies working with young people with a ready-made forum within which to contribute to a borough-wide strategy. This year's conference can be seen as a catalyst for future conferences in the Haringey area designed to find out what the needs of young people are; giving them a forum in which they can get their views heard; access information about resources, and have a valuable learning experience; and stimulating their thinking about strategies to survive in today's complex society.

Is the work written up and / or evaluated?

We provided an exit questionnaire which asked those who attended, how useful the day was, how best could agencies meet the needs of young people in the local community, and what they felt about the local education system, council services, police and housing services. The evaluation of these and other materials is still continuing, although an initial report is available from The Break-Free Project.

Contact: Khalid Abdul Karim Mair
Senior Project Worker
Break-Free Project
Selby Community Centre
1st Floor, South Block
Selby Road
London N17 8JN.
Tel. No: 0181-885-5000

Resources and further reading

Within this section, I have tried to find a balance between providing practitioners with a listing which is broad and inclusive of the many areas that we know workers are developing their practice within and one which they can use (i.e. highly selective). I have listed and described books, articles and resources that workers can use directly in their work and have also listed resources under work areas and groups of young men (e.g. black young men, and masculinity and offending). I have featured publications and packs that are recent enough to be of contemporary value. There are cross-references where appropriate and addresses from which books and resources are provided where they are not available via bookshops.

Background Reading

Men and Masculinity

Brod, Harry (Ed.) **The Making of Masculinities** (The new men's studies) *Allen & Unwin, London 1987.* A good range of essays covering aspects of men's studies. You will find theory, history, literature and research - its only weakness for some will be its academic style and approach.

Connell, Bob **Gender & Power Polity**, *Cambridge 1987.*

Connell, Bob **Masculinities Polity**, *Cambridge 1995.* Connell is an essential read for a thorough grounding in masculinities. He brought us a grasp of masculinities, and most of his work is well grounded in practice - Macquarie has developed some very good schools-based work. Again, these books are academic and a good grounding in sociology may be useful.

Edley, Neil and Wetherell, M. **Men in Perspective** (Practice, Power and Identity) *Prentice Hall, London 1995*. This is an excellent introduction to the area of gender, sexism and masculinity. Very accessible, it covers a lot of ground and is well-referenced into other literature. No real weaknesses, although the focus is on the social context, rather than the psychological or self!

Kilmartin, CT. **The Masculine Self** *MacMillan, New York 1994*. This is similar in form to Edley and Wetherall above, although its strengths are in the 'self', behaviours, beliefs, physical and mental health areas, as well as being a good broad-based introduction to masculinity.

Lloyd, Trefor and Wood, Tristan (Eds.) **What Next for Men?** *Working With Men, London 1996*. The 23 contributors were given 12 pages of statistics, trends and data about men and asked to write about how they understood this information and what they would do about it if they were 'Minister for Men'. The contributions are very varied, with some talking generally about men, and others taking specific groups and issues, such as black men or fatherhood.

Segal, Lynne **Slow Motion** (changing masculinities, changing men) *Virago, London 1990*. This is very well-written, accessible, but learned book that covers class and race very well. This alone makes it an essential read.

Young Men

Campbell, Bea **Goliath** (Britain's Dangerous Places) *Methuen, London 1993*. Bea Campbell takes the riots / disturbances of the early 80's to explore the interplay between masculinity, class, young men and the police, arguing that the 'young buck' and the 'boys in blue' are, in fact, two competing images of masculinity.

Eggerton, Peter et al. **Young Men Speaking Out** *Health Education Authority, London 1995*. One hundred and sixty interviews commissioned by the HEA with 16-20-year-old young men to help inform development of policy and practice. No great earth-shattering statements, but young men talking about feeling angry, frustrated or hopeless, violence, drugs, etc. Lots of quotes and some analysis.

Harland, Ken **Young Men Talking** (Voices from Belfast) *Working With Men, London 1997*. Twenty-five interviews with young men talking about school, work, the future, feelings, coping, asking for help, fathers and relationships. This book provides young men with an opportunity to talk about themselves, their lives and what they want, and sets out some practical responses.

Phillips, Angela **The Trouble With Boys** (parenting the men of the future) *Pandora, London 1993*. Seen by many as very influential in catching the mood of concern about young men, this book takes a psychosocial approach to the changing nature of society for young men. Alarmist, but informed, this is perceptive and full of journalistic pictures of the current state of being a man.

Black Men

Brown, Paul **'Working With Black Young Men setting out the difficulties'** in *Working With Men 1994 / 4* and **'Developing Work with Black Young Men survival, racism and masculinity'** in **Working With Men** 1995 / 1. Two articles that address both the problems and the possible solutions to developing work with young black men. The author describes examples of practice he has been involved in and implications on policy and developing practice.

Franklin, Clyde W. **'"Hey, Home Yo, Bro": Friendship Among Black Men'** in *Nardi, Peter M. Men's Friendships Sage, London 1992*. This is an excellent chapter in an excellent book. Explores the differences between working and middle-class black men's friendships, which the author suggests are differentiated by the need for survival and the needs for contacts and networking.

See Segal, Lynne (Men and Masculinity).

Gay Men

Frankum Jo **Young Gay Men Talking** AVERT, Horsham 1995. A small but very useful booklet that allows young gay men to talk for themselves.

Hall Carpenter Archives Gay Men's Oral History Group **Walking After Midnight** (Gay Men's Life Stories) Routledge, London 1989. A collection of 14 life stories from gay men of varying ages, focusing on personal experience within the context of meeting places, homophobia, the War and the Liberation Movements.

Trenchard, Lorraine and Warren, Hugh **Something to Tell You:** the experiences and needs of young lesbians and gay men in London London Gay Teenage Group, 1984. Getting very old now, but still a relevant account of gay men's and lesbians' lives and needs as the title suggests!

Men and Health

Bradford, Nikki **Men's Health Matters** (the complete A-Z of male health) Vermilion, London 1995. The cover tells us that this book "is an essential self-help directory for all men who want to take control of their health, find out more about their bodies and maximize their well-being, and for any woman that wants to understand them better". Sections each have sub-sections on 'what is it?', 'how common is it?', 'how do you catch it?', 'symptoms' and 'treatments'. This book incorporates within its approach an understanding of men and of the self-help model that men may respond to, and is written by a (good) journalist, so the style is very accessible.

Brewer, Sarah **The Complete Book of Men's Health** *Thorsens, London 1995.* The title is more than a bit misleading, as this book is primarily about sexual health. So, for example, 'the formation of sperm' gets 20 pages, while 'coronary heart disease' gets 10! The author has defined men's health as physiological and biological, and masculinity does not get a mention in the index, so this narrow definition limits the book enormously. However, this is very well written, even if the emphasis is on information - so you find out a lot about vitamins and minerals!

Lloyd, Trefor **Young Men's Health** (a youth work concern?) *Youth Action and Health Promotion Agency, Northern Ireland 1996.* This report describes both the process and the product of a young men's health initiative in Belfast, Northern Ireland. The emphasis is on the learning gained from the supporting of six short-term projects, what worked, what didn't, and the benefits gained by the workers and the young men. Also included are brief descriptions of the projects, a section on evaluation and a series of recommendation that would bring about further good examples of practice.

Lloyd, Trefor **Men's Health Review** *Royal College of Nursing, London 1996.* This literature review covers definitions of men's health, a discussion about whether men's health is determined by biological or behavioural factors, sexual health, heart disease, mental health, suicide and other literature produced since 1990. Also included are full references (for those wanting to use it as the start of a literature search) and a series of recommendation to address and enhance men's health issues.

Sabo D. & Gordon DF. **Men's Health and Illness** (Gender, power, and the body) *Sage, London 1995.* This is a good example of the very high quality of books in the 'Men and Masculinities' series edited by Michael Kimmel. The series of essays covers theoretical and research-based areas of men's health. The sleeve tells us that "this book thoroughly introduces readers to men's studies perspectives and their relevance for understanding men's health, while exploring linkages between traditional gender roles, men's health and larger structural and cultural contexts", and it's right!

See also Eggerton, Peter (Young Men).

Masculinity and Offending

Dominelli, Lena **Gender, Sex Offenders and Probation Practice** *Novata Press, 1991.* This covers the social construction of masculinity, its relevance to crime (and in particular to sexual violence) with a useful analysis of current probation practice. The Working With Men reviewer wrote "100 pages of succinct argument, references and no-nonsense style leaves you asking why the Probation Service has taken so long to face the fact that a serious perspective on gender has been sadly missing from the way it works with predominantly a male clientele" (WWM 1992 / 4).

Jenkins, Jan **Men, Masculinity and Offending** *ILPS and the London Action Trust, London 1994.* After a useful discussion on constructions of masculinity and the incidence of men and crime, the report details 10 projects working with men around the issues of offending and masculinity, and an in-depth evaluation of Camberwell Probation Centre. This very useful publication describes some of the most interesting work with men and provides an excellent set of starting points and ideas on how to develop similar work.

Lees, John and Lloyd, Trefor **Working With Men Who Batter Their Partners** *Working With Men, London 1994.* This booklet is designed as an introductory text, setting out the various theoretical perspectives, the core elements of programmes for such men, and various practice issues which projects have encountered. A list of current projects is given, as well as an annotated bibliography of further reading.

Newburn, Tim and Mair, George **Working With Men** *Russell House Publishing, Lyme Regis, Dorset 1996.* A collection of nine examples of practice within the criminal justice field, including domestic violence, car crime and masculinity and offending programmes.

Senior, Paul and Woodhill, David. **Gender, Crime and Probation Practice.** *PAVIC Publications, Sheffield City Polytechnic, Sheffield, 1992.* This is a collection of chapters from a number of perspectives, including 'Making Masculinity Explicit in Work with Male Offenders', 'Boys Don't Cry' and 'Empathy, Warmth, Collusion and Crime'. A good introduction to men and crime.

Sex Education and Sexual Health

Davidson, Neil **Boys Will Be...?** (Sex Education With Young Men) *Working With Men, London 1997. First published in 1990,* this has remained an essential guide for anyone developing work with young men within a sexual health context. This second edition has been substantially rewritten with the recent school sex education guidelines very much in mind.

Anti-Sexist Work

Cavanagh, Kate and Cree, Vivienne E. (Eds.) **Working With Men** (Feminism and Social Work) *Routledge, London 1995.* The editors argue that "feminist social work must address the issue of men: a refusal to do so may allow the expanding programme of 'men's work' within social work to proceed without a pro-feminist theoretical perspective and without an adequate understanding of women's experience".

See also Salisbury, Jonathan (Schools and the Curriculum).

Schools and the Curriculum

Browne, Rollo and Fletcher, Richard **Boys in School** (addressing the real issues behaviour, values and relationships) *Finch Publishing, Sydney, Australia 1995*. This collection reflects the rapidly-growing interest in work with young men in Australia. Contributors reflect on process, curriculum and behavioural issues, and provide a thought-provoking volume for anyone working in schools wanting to explore the impact of masculinity and gender and to develop strategies to deal with it.

Francis, Paul **Boys will be Men** *Shropshire Education Department, 1996*. This is a collection of teaching materials for use in PSE lessons in secondary schools, with the purpose being "to enable boys to think about themselves and their role, and to be more confident about how they might develop". Aimed at 14-16-year-olds, it details four hours of classroom assignment (divided into 'talking', 'reading' and 'research') for boy-only groups.

Salisbury, Jonathan and Jackson, David **Challenging Macho Values** (practical ways of working with adolescent boys) *Falmer Press, London 1996*. A resource book for teachers developing work with young men in school. The bulk of this book consists of theory and curriculum ideas across a number of issues, including sexuality, bullying and looking after yourself.

See also Mac an Ghaill, Mairtin (Sex, Sexuality and Homophobia).

Fatherhood

Augustus, Patrick **Baby Father 2** *The X Press, London 1995*. A great novel, it also has a lot to say about the range of attitudes about children, fathers and black men.

Bernard Van Leer Foundation Newsletter **Where have all the**

fathers gone? *No. 65 / January 1992.* This newsletter contains a number of well-written articles about fathering and projects in Jamaica, Scotland, New Mexico, South Africa and the Appellations.

Burgess, Adrienne **Fatherhood Reclaimed** (The making of the modern father) *Vermilion, London 1997.* This is a great book that will inform and stimulate. Starting with the history of fatherhood, the author goes on to look at the current and future position and role of fathers.

Burgess, Adrienne and Ruxton, Sandy **Men and Their Children** (Proposals for Public Policy) *Institute for Public Policy Research, 1996.* This is an excellent publication exploring the current situation for fathers and possible future policies. Covering supporting fathers, education, work, unmarried fathers and family breakdown, this is one of those rare documents that challenges your perspective - whatever it is.

Levine, James and Pitt, Edward **New Expectations** (community strategies for responsible fatherhood) *Families and Work Institute, New York 1995.* This is a very practical book, fronted with a theory and perspectives section (rethinking fatherhood), followed by a 'community strategies' section covering 'prevention', 'preparation', 'establishing programmes', 'involving fathers' and 'supporting fathers'. These sections all include examples of practice and policy implications. The last section details current American programmes and publications. Excellent for anyone thinking about setting up initiatives with fathers.

Levine, James **Getting Men Involved** (Strategies for early childhood programs) *Families and Work Institute, New York 1993.* This is targeted at those wanting to involve men within childcare settings and has sections on 'creating a father-friendly environment', 'recruiting men to your program', 'operating a fathers' program' and 'sustaining male involvement'. These sections are followed by thirteen 'model programs'. If you are thinking about involving men within a childcare setting, this is an essential and stimulating resource.

Marsiglio, William (Ed.) **Fatherhood** (Contemporary Theory, Research, and Social Policy) *Sage 'Research on Men and Masculinities Series', London, 1994*. Another book in this excellent Sage series, it covers both theoretical and policy issues.

Moss, Peter (Ed.) **Father Figures** (Fathers in the families of the 1990s) *HMSO / Children in Scotland, Edinburgh 1995*. This is a collection of talks given at a conference of the same name held in 1994. History, research, opinion and policy are all covered here, with Angela Phillips and Charlie Lewis among the speakers.

Sex, Sexuality and Homophobia

Chodorow, Nancy J. **Feminities, Masculinities, Sexualities** (Freud and Beyond) *Free Association Books, London 1994*. A provocative book, looking again at Freud's approach to sexuality (especially male sexuality). Nancy Chodorow attempts to separate male dominance and heterosexuality and rethinks the phychoanalytical approach that usually defines sexuality as 'normal' and 'abnormal'.

Holland, Janet, Ramazanoglu, Caroline and Sharpe, Sue **Wimp or Gladiator?** *Tufnell Press, 1993*. Based on a series of interviews with 16-21-year-old men which reflect the way that boys are drawn into exercising power over women, while at the same time being vulnerable to the possibilities of failure. This experience, the authors suggest, pressurises young men into sexual strategies which are based on subordinating women.

Mac an Ghaill, Mairtin **The Making of Men** (masculinities, sexualities and schooling) *Open University Press, Milton*

Keynes 1994. "Mairtin Mac an Ghaill explores how boys learn to be men in school whilst policing their own and others' sexualities. He focuses upon the students' confusions and contradictions in their gendered experiences; and upon how schools actively produce, through the official and hidden curriculum, a range of masculinities which young men come to inhabit". Academic in style, but lots of quotes from young men.

Redman, P. '**Curtis loves Ranjit**: heterosexual masculinities, schooling and pupils' sexual culture' in *Educational Review Vol. 48, 2 (1996).* A very interesting article that focuses on the transition between junior and secondary schools and its impact on the developing sexuality of boys.

Richardson, Diane (Ed.) **Theorising Heterosexuality** *Open University Press, Bucks. 1996.* A collection of essays that question the 'normality' of heterosexuality in terms of social and cultural identity. Academic, but very readable.

Wellings, Kaye, Field, Julia, Johnson, Anne M. and Wadsworth, Jane **Sexual Behaviour in Britain** (The National Survey of Sexual Attitudes and Lifestyles) *Penguin Books, London 1994.* Based on 20,000 responses, this book offers data on earliest sexual experiences, numbers of partners, sexual orientation, moral convictions and awareness of risk etc., etc., with a lot of statistics and graphs.

Resources, Packs, Videos and other Materials

Games

Grapevine Game -developed at the Grapevine Project for use with young people in year 7 and upwards. Board, dice and counters, with FACT and OPINION cards. Very good for assessing knowledge, and defining the subject areas that young people might want to cover. (National Youth Agency)

A Man's World -again, a board, dice and counter game, with FACT and OPINION cards that cover a wider range of issues around masculinity (including relationships, sexism, homophobia). For use with year 9 upwards. Very good for assessment and for involving young men in the game and discussing issues. (The B Team)

The Essence this board game raises issues about drug use, sexual activity and self-esteem. Aimed at increasing knowledge about sex and drugs, it will be useful for years 10 and 11 (some teachers may want to remove some of the 'bolder' sex cards). (Bread Youth Project)

Resources and Ideas Packs

Colours of the Rainbow (exploring issues of sexuality and difference) *Camden and Islington Community Health Services, 1996.* This is a resource for those in schools, including governors, parents and carers, wanting to affirm young gays and lesbians; encourage the recognition that there are young gays and lesbians within the school community; and give guidance for those wanting to include homophobia and heterosexuality within the curriculum. It consists of a very broad range of materials divided into sections (including the spectrum of sexuality and homophobia and its effects) for those from 5 years upwards.

Condom Teaching Model For Safer Sex is a model erect penis which can be used to practice putting on condoms. This one ejaculates so you get to remove the condom as well. (Adam Rouilly Ltd.)

FPA Contraceptive Display Kit contains samples of all the common types of contraception: pill, femidom, coils, condoms, etc. The Kit also has a useful booklet with a lot of information about the different contraceptives (such as their advantages and disadvantages) and some worksheets. (Family Planning Association)

Male and Female is a set of 15 laminated A4 cards with illustrations of male and female sexual organs, the process of fertilization and pregnancy. These are looking a bit dated now, but there is nothing to replace them. (Family Planning Association).

Male Image PhotoPack - 52 original 10" x 8" black and white photographs of men and boys that show men expressing a range of emotions and doing a number of activities. The PhotoPack will be of particular benefits for those workers looking for a resource to start a variety of discussions. (The B Team)

Him Book (Ideas for men looking at masculinity and sexism). Aimed at men's groups and workers with boys and men, this well-tried series of questionnaires and exercises is very useful in its own right, as well as a good stimulus for further ideas. (Sheffield City Libraries).

Taught not Caught (strategies for sex education) . This is a bit old, but still essential. It has a number of exercises on communication, relationships, decision-making, bodies, puberty, menstruation, contraception and sterilisation, pregnancy, birth, and STD's, and has a vast number of ideas and is very user-friendly, listing what you will need to carry through the exercises, including time, resources, space and aspects to look out for. (The Clarity Collective)

Testicular Self-Examination Trainer is a model of the scrotum and testicles, made from a soft material, which has two simulated tumours embedded in each testicle. A number of leaflets are available that show young men how to carry out TSE. (Adam Rouilly Ltd.)

The Equalizer 1 (Activity Ideas for Anti-sexist Youth Work) This pack is in two parts, the first introduces the context for working with young women and men about sexism and the second is given over to ten activity sessions, an evaluation sheet and a resources list. (Bread Youth Project)

The Equalizer II (Activity Ideas for empowerment work and anti-racist work with young people) 84 pages of ideas, questionnaires, games and roleplays for work on empowerment with young African-Caribbean people and for anti-racist work with young white people. Bread are renowned for their high quality and very well-tested resources (see Equalizer I and The Essence) and this is no different. What is particularly useful is the variety of reflective, knowledge and attitudinally-based exercises. Gender is a component in just two exercises, but this is still a very useful pack. (Bread Youth Project)

Alvarado, Scilla and Power, Paula **The Inside Story: Menstruation Education for Young Men and Women.** This pack has been prepared mainly for mixed environments, with some single- sex work. Although not essential, it is a very well thought-out resource.

Yerrell, Richard **Anti-sexist Practice with Boys & Young Men.** A resource pack of exercises & ideas. A series of questionnaires, exercises, games, quizzes and ideas listed under 'Being Male', 'Masculinity', 'Sexism', 'Sexuality' and 'Power and Violence'.

Videos

Everything you wanted to know about puberty....for boys *Disney Educational Productions (distributed by Viewtech Film & Video)*, 16 minutes. Aimed at 10-13-year-old boys, this drama shows two boys finding out about the physical, sexual and emotional changes they are going through. A very useful resource for those working with young men.

Sex: A guide for the young (*available from Educational Media International, 235 Imperial Drive, Rayners Lane, London HA2 7HE*). A Danish video (dubbed by a Canadian group) in cartoon format, explicitly showing a young man and woman having sex. Covers hygiene, homosexuality, orgasms, masturbation and sexual relationships in a humorous and real way. 20 minutes in length and available from EMI, .

Safe. A video about Young Black Men's Health. Produced in Birmingham, this has a storyline hingeing around the relationships between four young black men (one Asian and three African-Caribbean), living in a house owned by one of their parents, and covers sex, drugs, risk-taking, friendships and relationships The B Team.

Posters

Boyswork Posters are a set of 5, A1 black-and-white photographs with captions such as 'Why not show your feelings?', 'It's good to be close to your mates', 'Why do we men have to know all the answers?', 'What's to prove by fighting?'. (Available from The B Team)

Fatherhood is A Serious Business Posters is a set of 4, A2 posters showing fathers with their children. The set reflects Caribbean, Asian and European fathers. (Available from The B Team)

Spot the Heterosexual An A2 poster produced by North London Line showing 9 photographs of men and women.

Conclusions

Trefor Lloyd
Working With Men
320 Commercial Way
London SE15 1QN
Tel: and Fax: 0171-732-9409

Dear Reader,

Tradition says that conclusions are for telling the reader what you have already told them, and also to get in anything else you want to say before the light goes out! I have always thought you tell the reader what you have told them in the conclusion because you work on the basis that, in fact, the conclusion is likely to be the part of the book that the readers look at first or most.

So, for those readers who start with the conclusion, welcome! This book has tried to provide a broad perspective on work with boys and young men. It has argued that, todate, debates about young men have too often stopped at the "Aren't they a problem" juncture, and have failed to look at what we can, in fact, do if they are indeed a problem; while the literature on young men is relatively large, it is dominated by deep concern, high anxiety, fear and sometimes even loathing.

By addressing both the statistical and theoretical contexts, and looking to translate these into a practical model of understanding, this book has tried to indicate (and demonstrate through the examples of practice) ways in which we can develop work with boys and young men.

A number of underlying themes have run through the text.

One of the most important is the recognition of the rapidly-changing nature of the world for young people in general, and young men in particular. To often, we have looked at one half of this equation, focusing on either the effects on young people or the structural changes on our society. This leads us away from the most important component, which is the inter-relationship between the two. So this book has used as a backdrop both the dramatic changes and their impact on young men. As practitioners with young men, within our work role we have very little scope to impact on the societal changes, but we have to look at the impact these have on the young men we work with. In turn, we must address the need for young men to adapt to a rapidly-changing world that lacks clarity in terms of what it wants from its young people in general and young men in particular.

Another major theme throughout the book is that of being clear about what we are trying to do. Too often, work has developed on the basis of method and style, with workers arguing that "single sex environments" are what the work is about. Of course it isn't necessarily: we need to be clear about why we are doing what we are doing, and then methods and styles will fall into place. The clearer we are about purpose, the easier it will be to formulate outcomes and objectives and to carry through appropriate evaluation methods.

A third major theme is that of workers taking some responsibility for our current difficulties for developing good practice with young men. Too often, workers have externalised the problems as young men's inability to take opportunities offered to them, or young men's immaturity, inadequacy, resistance or inability to express themselves. While all of these can be factors in young men's difficulties in addressing issues, we have to accept that, as workers, we have had our own difficulties. Impatience, fear, annoyance, resentment and feelings of being threatened have all been barriers for workers in their attempts to work effectively with young men. More general stereotyped views of young men as being irresponsible, aggressive and reluctant to talk have also permeated work with boys and young men for both workers and the young men themselves. Any model of practice has to be based on a positive view of young men, even if challenge is not too far behind!

The fourth theme has been the centrality of masculinity in our understanding of young men. This book has placed masculinity (and particularly the early socialisation processes), in the middle of our understanding and our developing practice. This doesn't require an exclusivity or an argument that all other perspectives and viewpoints have less value, but it does require a thinking through and clarity about what the socialisation processes of masculinity are and what impact these have on young men, and, in turn, the implications these have on our developing practice. We can't ignore class, race, sexism, homophobia, able-bodiedism, or indeed adultism, by claiming that masculinity is the primary factor, but we also can't ignore its importance and the value this understanding can bring to our developing work.

Hopefully, as well as following through these different themes, this book will have met its most important objective - stimulating you to think both about the issues and your practice. Development of practice seems to occur best when workers are confident, stimulated and can see clear points of entry (and purpose) to what they are doing.

If this is the position this book has helped you reach, then it has succeeded in its purpose, and I wish you good luck in the development of your practice so that maybe, just maybe, young men will not have to be the final frontier.

Yours,

Trefor Lloyd
April 1997